Praying Daily:
A One Minute Scripture and Prayer

for each day of the year
as well as for special needs
and occasions

Emmie Leach

2

For Katie,
my beloved granddaughter
and friend

"The righteous flourish like the palm tree and grow like a cedar in Lebanon. They are planted in the house of the Lord; they flourish in the courts of our God. In old age they still produce fruit; they are always green and full of sap, showing that the Lord is upright; He is my rock, and there is no unrighteousness in Him."

Psalm 92:12 – 15

Preface

At 80 Mother decided she
wanted to start a new ministry.
And at 86 she continues her
work every day!

Having nursed her husband of
58 years through his final illness
and taken some time to travel
and listen to the Lord, she began
"A One Minute Daily Scripture
and Prayer," selecting a short
Bible verse and writing a prayer
around the wisdom of that
Scripture each day.

Using her computer, she records
in her own voice, with its gentle
Texas drawl, the Scripture and
prayer on her toll free number.
1.888.664.8792   Through
newspaper, prayer cards, visits
to local Churches, the ministerial
alliance and chance encounters
with people in restaurants, at
Walmart, in the line at the Post
Office, Mother shares her work
and invites others to join her in
prayer.

Through this book, she is inviting YOU to join your hearts with hers in prayer for your own needs, for the Churches, and for the whole world – especially for our sisters and brothers who are hurting.

On her desk where she studies and prays in preparation for writing her prayers is a stack of Bibles in many different versions. Mom goes most often to the Revised Standard Version but also uses the Amplified Version, the Revised New American Bible, the King James Version, the Living Bible, as well as the New International Version; once in a while some other translation pops into her view. Wherever she finds the Word of God most plainly communicated is her 'favorite' Bible at that moment.

Mother was raised in the Baptist Church, spent the years she was raising my brother and me with our dad in the Methodist Church, was then active for 20 years in the Assembly of God; most afternoons for 30 years she would join the nuns at the

6

Monastery of the Infant Jesus for Evening Prayer, and lately she has joyfully worshipped in the Episcopal Church. Mother has always said that she simply must follow Jesus, wherever He leads. This 'ecumenical' experience has created a broad outlook for Mother and made her love the Church wherever it meets.

When she was a child in the Baptist Church, she thought she heard the Lord calling her to be a missionary in China – like Lottie Moon. God's call to marriage and motherhood prevented Mom from ever getting to China as a missionary.

But she has ministered to thousands of people over the last 15 years through her two web sites.

CancerAndHealingPrayer.org
tells the story of her diagnosis with a usually fatal type of breast cancer when she was 49 and the prayer for healing which has sustained her every day since then. About that experience

Mother wrote her first book, "Twenty Years of Grace: Journeying through Cancer."

DepressionAndHealingPrayer.org is the story of Mother's lifelong struggle with depression and how the Lord heals her daily of that malady.

She invites you to visit her on the web at both of these sites for more insight into the ways God has lavished goodness and healing on her. And she wants to assure you that God desires those graces in abundance for you as well!

In 2015, because of the sage advice of her pastor at St Cyprian's Episcopal Church, Father Ralph Morgan, and with the help of Jordan Dietz, the youth minister there, Mom began posting her daily Scriptures and prayers on Facebook. You are most welcome to join her prayer community there:
Facebook.com/YourDailyPrayer

As you pray with Mom you will see that the Holy Spirit is often the focus of her intentions. And the Most Holy Trinity – Father, Jesus, and Holy Spirit – is frequently the way she understands God in her life. Very often these prayers reveal how much the Bible as the Word of God means to Mom.

These prayers also show that Mother is deeply concerned that we Christians respond to God's call throughout the Scriptures to take care of the oppressed, to seek God's healing power when we are sick, to see our faith as a perfect guide in the ways we vote and in the ways we use our time and money.

May this book of devotions for special needs and days, in addition to a prayer for each day of the year, bring you comfort and challenge with the assurance that my mom's prayers are happily joined with yours, for as Jesus promises us, "Where two or three gather in my

name, there am I with them."
(Matthew 18:20)

Reverend Monsignor Phillip
Meyer Leach, Jr., MSW, PhD
Emmie's older son

Contents

Scriptures and Prayers for each day of the year

Scriptures and Prayers for

January 1
Welcome to A One Minute
Daily Scripture and Prayer,
and may this be a very happy
new year for you!

In the Psalm 103, verse 1, we
read

"Bless the Lord, O my soul; and
all that is within me; bless His
holy name!"

Oh dear Lord, in this new year
give us every grace we need
truly to declare that our new
year's resolution is to give You
all that is in us and to spend our
lives each day in ways that
honor You!

We pray in the name of Jesus!

Amen

January 2
Welcome to A One Minute Daily Scripture and Prayer!

In the 1st chapter of Ezra, verses 5 & 6, we read

"Everyone whom God had inspired…prepared to go up to build the house of the Lord in Jerusalem. All their neighbors gave them help in every way, with silver and gold … besides all their free-will offerings."

Lord God, inspire us to help our neighbors, especially those who do not have adequate housing; let us use our silver and gold to help, in every way, those in need.

We pray in the name of Jesus!

Amen

January 3
Welcome to A One Minute Daily
Scripture and Prayer!

In the Psalm 91, verse 11, we
read

"God will command His angels
concerning you, to guard you in
all your ways."

Lord God, we lift up into Your
care all who travel this and every
day. Whether for business, for
pleasure, to visit family or
friends, or to return to their
homes, we ask that your holy
angels watch over all travelers.

We pray in the name of Jesus!

Amen

14

January 4

Welcome to A One Minute Daily Scripture and Prayer!

In the 6th chapter of Matthew, verse 34, we read

"Therefore, do not be anxious about tomorrow, for tomorrow will be anxious for itself. Let the day's own trouble be sufficient for the day."

Dear Lord, imprint into our minds and hearts this reassuring message so that we will not worry about what is in our future.

We pray in the name of Jesus, Who holds our future in His hands!

Amen

January 5
Welcome to A One Minute Daily
Scripture and Prayer!

In the 10th chapter of Mark,
verse 14, we read

"Jesus said, 'Let the children
come to me; do not hinder them,
for to such belongs the kingdom
of God!'"

Loving Jesus, we pray for all
children everywhere. We pray for
sick children, especially those in
hospitals; give them healing! We
pray for orphan children; give
them supportive and safe
homes! And we pray for children
who live in violent homes or war
zones; give them security and
peace!

We pray in Your name!

Amen

January 6

Welcome to A One Minute Daily Scripture and Prayer!

In the 8th chapter of First Kings, verses 17 & 18, we read

"My father David had it in mind to build a house for the name of the Lord, the God of Israel. But the Lord said to my father David, 'You did well to consider building a house for my name.'"

Even as You called David and Solomon to build a temple to Your honor in Jerusalem, Lord God, let us hear and respond to Your call to us to build our lives — our minds, hearts and bodies — into a living temple of Your Spirit.

We pray in Your name, Father!

Amen

January 7

Welcome to A One Minute Daily Scripture and Prayer!

In the 3rd chapter of Acts, verses 6 & 7, we read

"But Peter said, 'I have no silver or gold, but I give you what I have; in the name of Jesus Christ of Nazareth walk.' And he took him by the right hand and raised him up; and immediately his feet and ankles were strong.'"

Risen Lord, You empowered Peter to bring healing to a cripple man; fill us with Your Holy Spirit so that we can be agents of Your healing in the lives of people around us.

We pray in Your name, Jesus our Healer!

Amen

January 8
Welcome to A One Minute Daily
Scripture and Prayer!

In the 4th chapter of Acts, verse
4, we read

"But many of those who heard
the word believed; and the
number of the men came to
about five thousand."

Lord Jesus, when we speak
about You and Your resurrection
and trust Your Holy Spirit to
open the hearts of those who
hear, we know that people will
come to believe in You. Give us
courage to proclaim the Good
News to all with whom we come
into contact.

We pray, asking the Holy Spirit
to lead us every day!

Amen

January 9

Welcome to A One Minute Daily Scripture and Prayer!

In the 1st chapter of First Peter, verse 3, we read

"Blessed be the God and Father of our Lord Jesus Christ! By his great mercy we have been born anew to a living hope through the resurrection of Jesus Christ from the dead."

Thank You, Father, for Your great mercy to all of us which gives us hope. Because Jesus rose from the dead and because we have been born anew to live forever with him, we have confidence and trust in the good times of life and in our trials!

We pray in the name of Jesus, our risen Lord!

Amen

January 10
Welcome to A One Minute Daily
Scripture and Prayer!

In Psalm 149, verse 4a, we read

"The Lord delights in his people."

Thank You, Lord, that even
though we are far from perfect,
You look on us as we are, and
You accept us and love us. Help
us to live our lives each day as
You would have us to, with love
for You and for our neighbors.

We pray in Your name, Lord of
Love!

Amen

January 11
Welcome to A One Minute Daily
Scripture and Prayer!

In the 1st chapter of First Peter,
verse 8, we read

"Without having seen him you
love him; though you do not now
see him you believe in him and
rejoice with unutterable and
exalted joy."

We marvel, Lord God, at the
great mercy You bestow on us
who — though we have not seen
Jesus in the flesh — believe in
Him and love Him. Fill us today,
and all the days of our lives, with
that indescribable and glorious
joy which He brings.

We pray in the name of Jesus,
the source of our joy!

Amen

January 12
Welcome to A One Minute Daily
Scripture and Prayer!

In the 24th chapter of Luke,
verses 15 & 16, we read

"While they were talking and
discussing together, Jesus
himself drew near and went with
them. But their eyes were kept
from recognizing him."

Lord Jesus, thank You for
meeting us along our ways, even
when our eyes are kept from
recognizing You. Help us to see
You in the people we encounter,
in the nature which surrounds
us, in the outcast, and in
opportunities for serving the
poor.

We pray in Your name, Lord
Jesus Who call us to love all!

Amen

January 13

Welcome to A One Minute Daily
Scripture and Prayer!

In the 24th chapter of Luke,
verses 47 & 48, we read

"Repentance and forgiveness of
sins should be preached in
Jesus' name to all nations,
beginning from Jerusalem. You
are witnesses of these things."

Lord Jesus, You told Your
followers to go and preach
the good news of repentance
and forgiveness, available to all
people. Help us to be examples
of this truth; send men and
women to all the earth to
proclaim Your love!

We pray in Your name, loving
Lord!

Amen

January 14
Welcome to A One Minute Daily
Scripture and Prayer!

In the 1st chapter of Acts, verses
6 & 7, we read

"So when they had come
together, they asked Jesus,
'Lord, will you at this time restore
the kingdom of Israel?' He said
to them, 'It is not for you to know
times or seasons which the
Father has fixed by his
authority.'"

Lord Jesus, when I want to know
what will happen in the future,
help me to be at peace in the
sure knowledge that our Father
in heaven orders all things for
our good.

We pray in Your name!

Amen

January 15

Welcome to A One Minute Daily Scripture and Prayer!

In the 16th chapter of Mark, verses 16 - 18, we read

"He who believes and is baptized will be saved…. And these signs will accompany those who believe: in my name they will cast out demons; they will speak in new tongues; they will pick up serpents, and if they drink any deadly thing, it will not hurt them; they will lay their hands on the sick, and they will recover."

Thank You, Lord, that I believe this scripture and know it is true for I have seen it happen at times. Let each of us live so close to You that You can guide us when You want us to be used in these miraculous ways.

We pray in the name of Jesus!

Amen

January 16
Welcome to A One Minute
Daily Scripture and Prayer!

In the 28th chapter of Matthew,
verses 1 & 2, we read

"Now after the sabbath, toward
the dawn of the first day of the
week, Mary Magdalene and the
other Mary went to see the
sepulcher. And behold there was
a great earthquake; for the angel
of the Lord descended from
heaven and came and rolled
back the stone, and sat upon it."

O Lord, when we are frightened
by storms, loud thunder, cracks
of lightening, and other unusual
things around us, help us to
remember that You are our
security and protection.

We pray in Your name, Lord of
the universe!

Amen

January 17

Welcome to A One Minute Daily
Scripture and Prayer!

In the 28th chapter of Matthew,
verses 5 & 6, we read

"But the angel said to the
women. 'Do not be afraid;
for I know that you seek Jesus
who was crucified. He is not
here; for he has risen as he said.
Come, see the place where he
lay.'"

Lord, open our eyes and hearts
so we can see the angels You
send to us and not be afraid -
people who speak words of
comfort, offer us help and advice
or give us a smile when we are
down. Thank You for lifting us up
through them!

We pray in Your name, Lord!

Amen

January 18

Welcome to A One Minute Daily
Scripture and Prayer!

In the 28th chapter of Matthew,
verses 9 & 10, we read

"And behold, Jesus met them
and said, 'Hail!' And they came
up and took hold of his feet and
worshiped Him. Then Jesus said
to them, 'Do not be afraid; go
and tell my brethren to go to
Galilee, there they will see me.'"

Dear Lord Jesus, today if You
appear to us, help us not to
be afraid; rather, let us be so
thrilled to see You that we will
reach out to you and worship
you and hear to you speak to us;
let us always be quick to do
whatever you tell us to do.

We pray in Your name!

Amen

January 19

Welcome to A One Minute Daily
Scripture and Prayer!

In the 28th chapter of Matthew,
verses 12 & 13, we read

"And when they had assembled
with the elders and taken
council, they gave a sum of
money to the soldiers and said,
'Tell people, 'His disciples came
by night and stole him away
while we were asleep.'"

Oh Lord, when those who are in
authority decide to tell lies in
order to protect themselves, their
lies harm Your people
everywhere. Give our leaders
courage and determination to tell
the Truth.

We pray in the name of Jesus,
Who is the Truth.

Amen

January 20

Welcome to A One Minute Daily Scripture and Prayer!

In the 20th chapter of John, verses 11 - 13, we read

"But Mary stood weeping outside the tomb; and as she wept she stooped to look into the tomb; and she saw two angels in white sitting where the body of Jesus had lain, one at the head and one at the feet. They said to her, 'Woman, why are you weeping?' She said to them, 'Because they have taken away my Lord, and I do not know where they have laid him.'"

Lord Jesus, when we grieve because we have lost loved ones, help us to be comforted that, because You died and rose, we, too, have that same hope of resurrection for those we love.

We pray in Your name, Risen Lord!

Amen

January 21

Welcome to A One Minute Daily
Scripture and Prayer!

In the 20th chapter of John,
verses 14 & 15, we read

"Saying this, she turned round
and saw Jesus standing there,
but she did not know that it was
Jesus. He said to her, 'Woman,
why are you weeping? Whom do
you seek?' Supposing him to be
the gardener, she said to him,
'Sir, if you have carried him
away, tell me where you have
laid him, and I will take him
away.'"

Dear Lord, help us who know
You, to persevere in our search
to know You better, and help us
to recognize when You are
speaking to us.

We pray in Your name, Lord
Jesus!

Amen

January 22

Welcome to A One Minute Daily
Scripture and Prayer!

In the 20th chapter of John, verses
16 - 18, we read

"Jesus said to her, 'Mary!' She
turned and said to him in Hebrew
'Rabbouni (which means Teacher).'
Jesus said to her, 'Do not hold me,
for I have not yet ascended to the
Father; but go to my brethren and
say to them, 'I ascending to my
Father, to my God and your God.'
Mary Magdalene went and said to
the disciples 'I have seen the Lord;'
and she told them that he had said
these things to her."

Lord, help us to be like Mary
Magdalene and to follow You
no matter what others say. Give us
confidence that You will give Your
message to us so that we can
deliver it to others.

We pray in Your name, Lord Jesus!

Amen

January 23

Welcome to A One Minute Daily
Scripture and Prayer!

In the 20th chapter of John,
verses 28 & 29, we read

"Thomas answered Jesus, 'My
Lord and my God!' Jesus said to
him, 'Have you believed because
you have seen me? Blessed are
those who have not seen and yet
believe.'"

Thank You Lord Jesus, that You
have given all of us who have
not seen You with our eyes the
wonderful blessing of choosing
to believe in You as our Lord and
Savior!

We pray, Jesus, with gratitude
for Your many gifts to us!

Amen

January 24
Welcome to A One Minute Daily
Scripture and Prayer!

In the 21st chapter of John,
verses 4 - 6, we read

"Just as day was breaking,
Jesus stood on the beach; yet
the disciples did not know that it
was Jesus. He said to them,
'Children, have you any fish?'
They answered, 'No.' He said to
them, 'Cast the net on the right
side of the boat, and you will find
some.' So they cast it, and now
they were not able to haul it in
for the quantity of the fish."

Lord, when have many burdens,
come to us as You did to the
disciples and show us how best
to manage them; give us wisdom
always to follow Your advice.

We pray in Your all-knowing
name, Lord Jesus!

Amen

January 25

Welcome to A One Minute Daily
Scripture and Prayer!

In the 21st chapter of John,
verses 12 - 14, we read

"Jesus said to the disciples,
'Come and have breakfast.' Now
none of the disciples dared to
ask him 'Who are you?' They
knew it was the Lord. Jesus
came and took the bread and
gave it to them, and so with the
fish. This was now the third time
that Jesus was revealed to the
disciples after he was raised
from the dead."

How wonderful to see Your care,
Risen Lord Jesus, by making
breakfast for Your disciples and
feeding them after You were
raised from the dead. Give us
hope that we will, one day, see
those we have lost & recognize
them as Your disciples.

We pray in Your Name, Risen
Lord!

Amen

January 26

Welcome to A One Minute Daily
Scripture and Prayer!

In the 21st chapter of John,
verses 15, we read

"When they had finished
breakfast, Jesus said to Simon
Peter, 'Simon, son of John, do
you love me more than these?'
He said to him, 'Yes Lord; you
know that I love you.' Jesus said
to him, 'Feed my lambs.'"

Lord, give us courage always to
help us to hear Your words and
then to act on them so that we,
too, will feed Your sheep.

We pray in the name of the
Good Shepherd, Who is Jesus!

Amen

January 27

Welcome to A One Minute Daily Scripture and Prayer!

In the 11th chapter of Isaiah, verse 2, we read

"The spirit of the Lord shall rest upon him: a spirit of wisdom and of understanding, a spirit of counsel and of strength, a spirit of knowledge and of fear of the Lord."

Lord Holy Spirit, fill us with a proper fear of You so that we will be eager to receive Your strength and wisdom to guide our interactions with others. Rather than judging people, let us be understanding, gracious and kind toward all.

We pray in the name of Jesus!

Amen

January 28
Welcome to A One Minute Daily
Scripture and Prayer!

In the 12th chapter of First
Corinthians, verse 13, we read

"It was in one Spirit that all of us,
whether Jew or Greek, slave or
free, were baptized into one
body. All of us have been given
to drink of the one Spirit."

Lord God, You have graciously
poured out Your Holy Spirit
on people of every nation and
tongue. And so, all of us who
share in that one Spirit are
sisters and brothers. By the
power of Your Spirit in us, allow
our prejudice and fear to be
overcome, so that we will reach
out in love to all people
everywhere.

We pray in the name of Jesus!

Amen

January 29

Welcome to A One Minute Daily
Scripture and Prayer!

In the 5th chapter of Acts, verses
30 - 32, we read

"The God of our ancestors raised
Jesus…. God exalted Him
at His right hand as leader and
savior…. We are witnesses of
these things, as is the Holy Spirit
Whom God has given to
those who obey Him."

Thank You, Lord God, for raising
Jesus from the dead, for exalting
Him at Your right hand, and for
sending the Holy Spirit to us!
Make us obedient servants who
happily share our faith and gladly
witness to Your glory before all
people.

We pray in the Name of the
Risen Jesus!

Amen

January 30

Welcome to A One Minute Daily Scripture and Prayer!

In the 1st chapter of Acts, verses 4 - 6, we read

"They were all filled with the Holy Spirit and began to speak in different tongues as the Spirit enabled them to proclaim… there were Jews from every nation under heaven… but they were confused because each one heard them speaking in his own language."

Lord Holy Spirit, Your mighty and miraculous works are often confusing to our limited human minds. Expand our horizons to recognize the grandeur of Your ways; do not let our pettiness prevent us from seeing Your majesty!

We pray in the name of Jesus!

Amen

January 31
Welcome to A One Minute Daily
Scripture and Prayer!

In the 4th chapter of Ephesians,
verses 30 - 32, we read

"Do not grieve the Holy Spirit of
God, with Whom you were
sealed… Get rid of all bitterness,
fury, anger, shouting… And be
kind…, compassionate and
forgiving."

Lord God, thank You for sealing
Your gifts of kindness,
compassion & forgiveness in our
lives by the power of Your Holy
Spirit. When we hold onto
bitterness & anger, when we
shout at family, co-workers or
strangers, let Your Spirit calm us
& give us peace.

We pray in the name of Jesus!

Amen

February 1
Welcome to A One Minute Daily
Scripture and Prayer!

In the 12th chapter of Mark,
verses 32b & 33, we read

"You are right, Teacher; you
have truly said that God is one,
and there is no other but he; and
to love him with all the heart, and
with all understanding, and with
all the strength, and to love one's
neighbor as oneself, is much
more important than all whole
burnt offerings and sacrifices."

God of love, enter into our minds
and hearts; help us to
understand that to love You
above all earthly riches and
treasures is Your desire for each
of us and that You call us to love
our neighbors.

We pray in Your name, God of
Love!

Amen

February 2
Welcome to A One Minute Daily
Scripture and Prayer!

In the 14th chapter of Romans,
verses 17 & 19, we read

"For the kingdom of God is not a
matter of food or drink, but of
righteousness, peace, and joy in
the Holy Spirit…. Let us then
pursue what leads to peace and
to building up one another."

Lord Holy Spirit, give us Your joy
so that we will want to build one
another up; make our own lives
more righteous and just so that
we can help to bring Your
Kingdom of peace to the whole
world.

We pray in the name of Jesus!

Amen

February 3
Welcome to A One Minute Daily
Scripture and Prayer!

In the 33rd chapter of Job, verse
4, we read

"For the Spirit of God has made
me, the breath of the Almighty
keeps me alive."

Help us to recognize, Lord God,
in every living being a creature
made by Your Spirit. By the
power of Your Holy Spirit, give
us the generosity of heart to care
for all those created by You,
without counting the cost.

We pray in the name of Jesus!

Amen

February 4

Welcome to A One Minute Daily Scripture and Prayer!

In the 4th chapter of Zechariah, verse 6, we read

"This is the word of the Lord to Zerubbabel: 'Not by might, nor by power, but by my spirit, says the Lord of hosts.'"

Lord, send Your Holy Spirit upon us so He can show us that all our human power and apparent knowledge will not make us happy or fully content. Help us to put the Holy Spirit in charge of our own lives so that He will meet our truest needs.

We pray in His mighty name!

Amen

February 5
Welcome to A One Minute Daily
Scripture and Prayer!

In the 1st chapter of Acts, verse
8, we read

"But you shall receive Power
when the Holy Spirit has come
upon you; and you shall be my
witnesses in Jerusalem and in all
Judea, and to the end of the
earth."

O Lord, I do so need Power in
my life to be a strong witness to
Your goodness. Send Your Holy
Spirit on me so that He will make
me witness to my family, friends,
town and to the end of the earth
in loving, truthful and respectful
ways.

We pray in the name of Jesus!

Amen

February 6

Welcome to A One Minute Daily Scripture and Prayer!

In the 5th chapter of Galatians, verses 22 & 23, we read

"But the fruit of the Spirit is love, joy, peace, patience, kindness, goodness, faithfulness, gentleness, self-control; against such there is no law."

O Lord, help us to see that when we are filled with Your Holy Spirit and live daily close to Him, He produces in us the precious fruits of love, joy, peace and all the other gifts promised in the Bible. Let us live with Him and in Him so that, by His Presence in us, we will be led to lives that are beautiful and meaningful.

We pray, Father, asking You to fill us with Your Holy Spirit!

Amen

February 7
Welcome to A One Minute Daily
Scripture and Prayer!

In the 5th chapter of Galatians,
verses 24 - 26, we read

"And those who belong to Christ
Jesus have crucified the flesh
with its passions and desires. If
we live by the Spirit, let us also
walk by the Spirit. Let us have no
self-conceit, no provoking of one
another, no envy of one
another."

Dear Holy Spirit, give me the
strength to want to be completely
Yours and to want nothing but
whatever You call me to be and
to do. Give me the will to crucify
my passions and desires to get
the better of people or to put
them down; rid me of envy and
jealousy. Make me, Lord, Yours!

We pray in Your name!

Amen

February 8

Welcome to A One Minute Daily
Scripture and Prayer!

In the 3rd chapter of Matthew,
verses 16 & 17, we read

"And when Jesus was baptized,
he went up immediately from the
water and behold the heavens
were opened and he saw the
Spirit of God descending like a
dove, and alighting on him; and,
lo, a voice from heaven saying,
'This is my beloved Son, with
whom I am well pleased.'"

Father, You sent the Holy Spirit
to rest on Jesus at his baptism,
and You proclaimed Him as Your
beloved Son. Help us to see
Jesus each day and in every
person and circumstance and,
so, be even more devoted to him
because You love Him so much.

We pray in Your name, Father!

Amen

February 9
Welcome to A One Minute Daily
Scripture and Prayer!

In the 5th chapter of Romans,
verse 5, we read

"And hope does not disappoint
us, because God's love has
been poured into our hearts
through the Holy Spirit which has
been given to us."

O Lord, through Your gift of the
Holy Spirit living in us, we have
Your love. Pour out the Holy
Spirit into our hearts so that we
can experience Your love more
deeply every day and so that we
can share that divine love with
each person with whom we
come into contact.

We pray in Your Holy name!

Amen

February 10

Welcome to A One Minute Daily Scripture and Prayer!

In the 8th chapter of Romans, verses 5 & 6, we read

"For those who live according to the flesh set their minds on the things of the flesh, but those who live according to the Spirit set their minds on the things of the Spirit. To set the mind on the flesh is death, but to set the mind on the Spirit is life and peace."

O Lord, give me every grace I need to let go of all the worldly endeavors that tempt me to move away from You, and set my mind on the things of the Holy Spirit, so I will receive the full life and peace that He produces in me each day!

We pray in Your name!

Amen

February 11
Welcome to A One Minute Daily
Scripture and Prayer!

In the 8th chapter of Romans,
verse 11, we read

"If the Spirit of him who raised
Jesus from the dead dwells in
you, he who raised Christ Jesus
from the dead will give life to
your mortal bodies also through
his Spirit which dwells in you."

O Lord, give us faith that when
we have invited the Holy Spirit to
live in us while we are alive, He
will give life to our mortal bodies
when we die — just as He did for
Jesus when He died.

We pray in the name of Jesus,
through the mighty power of the
Holy Spirit!

Amen

February 12

Welcome to A One Minute Daily
Scripture and Prayer!

In the 8th chapter of Romans,
verses 14 & 15, we read

"For all who are led by the Spirit
of God are sons of God. For you
did not receive the spirit of
slavery to fall back into fear, but
you have received the spirit
of sonship."

Lord Jesus, help us to believe
that we, who have received Your
Holy Spirit, do not need to be
fearful of things in life that seem
scary – for we are Your children,
Your sons and daughters, and
we can be completely confident
that You will protect us from
harm and that You are with us in
trials.

We pray in Your holy name,
Lord!

Amen

February 13
Welcome to A One Minute Daily
Scripture and Prayer!

In the 8th chapter of Romans,
verses 16 & 17, we read

"When we say, 'Abba! Father!' it
is the Spirit himself bearing
witness with our spirit that we are
children of God, and if children,
then heirs, heirs of God and
fellow heirs with Christ provided
we suffer with him in order that
we may also be glorified with
him."

Thank You, dear Lord, for the gift
of Your Holy Spirit Who speaks
to us deep in our hearts and tells
us that we really are Your
children, heirs of God. As Your
children, we now have all the
treasures, peace, security, and
power to overcome trials, which
You have given through Your
Son Jesus.

We pray in the name of Jesus,
our Brother!

Amen

February 14

Welcome to A One Minute Daily Scripture and Prayer!

In the 8th chapter of Romans, verse 26, we read

"Likewise the Spirit helps us in our weakness; for we do not know how to pray as we ought, but the Spirit himself intercedes for us with sighs too deep for words."

Dear Holy Spirit, help us, as we pray, to ask You to intercede for us and for all those we love, for Your prayers are always perfect and wise. Because Your prayers go deep and touch the very most important issues in our lives, we trust You for ourselves and for those we love.

We pray in Your Holy name!

Amen

February 15
Welcome to A One Minute Daily
Scripture and Prayer!

In the 8th chapter of Romans,
verse 27, we read

"And he who searches the hearts
of men knows what is the mind
of the Spirit, because the Spirit
intercedes for the saints
according to the will of God."

Heavenly Father, You search our
minds and know our hearts;
thank you that Your Holy Spirit,
living in us, intercedes for us
according to Your will and
through the Spirit's intercession
on our behalf, we know that our
prayers are pleasing to You.

We pray in Your name, Heavenly
Father!

Amen

February 16

Welcome to A One Minute Daily
Scripture and Prayer!

In the 8th chapter of Romans,
verse 28, we read

"We know that in everything God
works for good with those who
love him, who are called
according to his purpose."

Lord God, give us every grace
we need to trust You in both
good times and in bad times
because we have put You in
charge of our lives and You will
work all things together for our
good!

We pray in Your mighty name!

Amen

February 17
Welcome to A One Minute Daily
Scripture and Prayer!

In the 8th chapter of Romans,
verses 31 & 32, we read

"What then shall we say to this?
If God is for us, who is against
us? He who did not spare his
own Son but gave him up for us
all, will he not also give us all
things with him?"

O Lord, we are amazed that You
love us so deeply and care for
our every concern! Thank You
that Your love is so profound and
that You shower us with gifts of
faith, forgiveness, and protection
which Jesus, Your Son, won for
us on the cross.

We pray in the name of Jesus!

Amen

February 18

Welcome to A One Minute Daily
Scripture and Prayer!

In the 8th chapter of Romans,
verses 38 & 39, we read

"For I am sure that neither death,
nor life, nor angels, nor
principalities, nor things present,
nor things to come, nor powers,
nor height, nor depth, nor anything else in all creation, will be
able to separate us from the love
of God in Christ Jesus our Lord."

O Lord, give us every grace we
need to live each day with peace
and to face whatever comes,
secure in the protection of Your
loving arms.

We pray in the name of Jesus,
our strong Savior!

Amen

60

February 19
Welcome to A One Minute Daily
Scripture and Prayer!

In the 10th chapter of Romans,
verses 9 - 11, we read

"Because, if you confess with
your lips that Jesus is Lord and
believe in your heart that God
raised him from the dead you will
be saved. For man believes with
his heart and so is justified, and
he confesses with his lips and so
is saved. The scripture says, 'No
one who believes in him will be
put to shame.'"

Lord Jesus, thank You that You
have given us the way to
salvation. Move in the lives of all
those who have not accepted
you and bring them to You.

We pray in Your name, Savior of
the world!

Amen

February 20

Welcome to A One Minute Daily
Scripture and Prayer!

in the 11th chapter of Romans
verses 33 & 36, we read

"O the depth of the riches and
wisdom and knowledge of God!
How unsearchable are his
judgments and how inscrutable
his ways! For from Him and
through Him and to Him are all
things. For all things originate
with Him and come from Him; all
things live through Him, and all
things center in and tend to
consummate and to end in Him.
To Him be glory forever. Amen."

Thank You, Lord, that we can
put our trust in You for You alone
know all things and from You all
things are. Please, O God, give
us the peace and calm which
come from putting our trust in
You.

We pray in Your name, Lord of
the universe!

Amen

February 21

Welcome to A One Minute Daily Scripture and Prayer!

In the 12th chapter of Romans, verses 1 & 2, we read

"I appeal to you therefore, brethren, by the mercies of God, to present your bodies as a living sacrifice holy and acceptable to God, which is your spiritual worship. Do not be conformed to the world but be transformed by the renewal of your mind, that you may prove what is the will of God, what is good and acceptable and perfect."

O Lord, renew our minds so that we can see how different are Your ways from the ways that occupy people consumed by the busy-ness of the world. Help us to want to be all Yours and to give You our all and to live each day in Your perfect will, worshipping You with our whole being.

We pray in Your Holy name!

Amen

February 22

Welcome to A One Minute Daily
Scripture and Prayer!

In the 12th chapter of Romans,
verses 9 -11, we read

"Let love be genuine, hate what
is evil, hold fast to what is good;
love one another with brotherly
affection; out-do one another in
showing honor. Never flag in
zeal, be aglow with the Spirit,
serve the Lord."

Dear Lord of Love, give each of
us the graces we need to
live daily showing our love for
family, friends, and each person
we encounter by acts of
kindness and affection. Let
others see You when they see
us.

We pray in the name of Jesus,
Who is love!

Amen

February 23

Welcome to A One Minute Daily Scripture and Prayer!

In the 6th chapter of Ephesians, verse 15, we read

"And having shod your feet with the equipment of the gospel of peace;"

Help us, Lord, in our daily work to be preachers of the Good News which brings peace in our lives and peace with God. Help us to share better our message of Your love with other people.

We pray in the name of Jesus, Who is the Good News!

Amen

February 24

Welcome to A One Minute Daily Scripture and Prayer!

In Psalm 101, verse 5, we read

"One who secretly slanders a neighbor I will destroy. A haughty look and an arrogant heart I will not tolerate."

O Lord, help us to walk away from those who speak false rumors about others and refuse to listen to their lies and gossip, but, rather, help us always to defend those who are talked about untruthfully. Give us humble hearts that have no place for or desire to be with the haughty arrogant in the world.

We pray in the name of Jesus, our Example of courage, truth and love!

Amen

February 25
Welcome to A One Minute Daily
Scripture and Prayer!

In the 3rd chapter of First John,
verses 2 & 3, we read

"Beloved, we are God's children
now; it does not yet appear what
we shall be, but we know that
when Jesus appears we shall be
like Him, for we shall see Him as
He is. And everyone who thus
hopes in Him, purifies himself as
He is pure."

Lord Jesus, give us strong faith
in the sure and certain
knowledge that we are Your
children now; purify us so we will
be more and more like You
every day.

We pray in Your name, Savior!

Amen

February 26

Welcome to A One Minute Daily Scripture and Prayer!

In the 1st chapter of Isaiah, verses 18 - 20, we read

"Come now, let us reason together, says the Lord. Though your sins are like scarlet, they shall be as white as snow; though they are red as crimson, they shall be like wool. If you are willing and obedient, you will eat the best from the land; but if you resist and rebel you will be devoured by the sword. For the mouth of the Lord has spoken."

Lord, You call us to reason with You and You offer us forgiveness of our sins, even the worst of sins. Help us to be willing and obedient and so enjoy all the good things that You offer.

We pray in Your name, Lord of the universe!

Amen

February 27
Welcome to A One Minute Daily
Scripture and Prayer!

In Psalm 146, verse 9, we read

"The Lord protects the foreigners
among us. He cares for the
orphans and widows, but he
frustrates the plans of the
wicked."

O Lord, soften the hearts of all
those in our nation who are not
welcoming to oppressed people
from other nations. Help us to
accept Your call to us so that we
will become more like You, Who
care for orphans and widows.

We pray in Your name, Lord of
all nations!

Amen

February 28
Welcome to A One Minute Daily
Scripture and Prayer!

In the 2nd chapter of Philippians,
verses 3 & 4, we read

"Do nothing out of selfish
ambition or vain conceit, but in
humility consider others better
than yourselves. Each of you
should look not only to your own
interests, but also to the interests
of others."

O God, help us to bow down on
our knees and humbly ask You
to forgive our selfishness, and to
widen our concern for the poor,
the helpless, and the needy. May
we see the needs of others and
help them by praying for them
and by sharing our wealth with
them.

We pray in Your name generous,
Lord!

Amen

February 29
Welcome to A One Minute Daily
Scripture and Prayer!

In the 4th chapter of Philippians,
verse 8, we read

"Finally, brothers, whatever is
true, whatever is noble, whatever
is right, whatever is pure,
whatever is lovely, whatever is
admirable—if anything is
excellent or praiseworthy—think
about such things."

Dear Lord, imprint on our minds
and hearts these words of
scripture so that when we are
constantly bombarded with
sounds on the tv and people who
tell untruths, we will shut them
off from our ears and turn our
thinking to things that are
excellent and praiseworthy.

We pray in the name of Jesus,
our strong and merciful Lord!

Amen

March 1

Welcome to A One Minute Daily
Scripture and Prayer!

In the 1st chapter of Isaiah,
verse 17, we read

"Learn to do good, seek justice,
encourage the oppressed.
Defend the cause of the
fatherless, plead the case of the
widow."

Lord, inspire us to want to do
good. When we see our
neighbors and our nation
growing further away from being
just, send us leaders who will
stand for the rights of orphans
and widows, and move within us
so that we will want to work each
day to bring a more just and
caring world into being.

We pray in Your name, Just
Lord!

Amen

March 2

Welcome to A One Minute Daily Scripture and Prayer!

In Psalm 12 verses, 2 - 6, we read

"Neighbors lie to each other speaking with flattering lips and deceitful hearts. May the Lord cut off their flattering lips and silence boastful tongues. They say, 'We will lie to our hearts content. Our lips are our own - who can stop us?' The Lord replies, 'I have seen violence done to the helpless and I will rise up to rescue them as they have longed for me to do.'"

O Lord, when the lies of men and women fill the air and they arrogantly continue to lie, help us to turn our thoughts and prayers to You because You alone have the power to rescue us from the harm they do.

We pray in Your mighty name!

Amen

March 3

Welcome to A One Minute Daily Scripture and Prayer!

In the 1st chapter of Second Corinthians, verses 3 & 4, we read

"Blessed be the God and Father of our Lord Jesus Christ, the Father of mercies and God of all comfort, who comforts us in our afflictions so that we may be able to comfort those who are in any affliction with the comfort with which we ourselves are comforted by God."

Thank You, Father, for all the many times You have come to me, and to others, when we have been in trouble, showering us with Your love and care. Give us strength and courage to offer to all who are suffering our love, prayers and presence as You do for us.

We pray in Your name, loving Father!

Amen

March 4

Welcome to A One Minute Daily
Scripture and Prayer!

In the 2nd chapter of Galatians,
verses 19 & 20, we read

"For it was through the reading
of the Scriptures that I came to
realize that I could never find
God's favor by trying—and
failing—to obey the laws. I came
to realize that acceptance with
God came by believing in Christ.
I have been crucified with Christ:
and I myself no longer live, but
Christ lives in me. And the real
life I now have within this body is
a result of trusting in the Son of
God, who loved me and gave
Himself for me."

Lord, give us strength to let go of
all our worldly ways so that
You can fill us with Your
Presence. Let us be all Yours
and trust You each day to guide
our every thought word and deed
so that others will see You in us.

We pray in Your name, Lord!

Amen

March 5

Welcome to A One Minute Daily
Scripture and Prayer!

In the 18th chapter of Matthew,
verses 3 & 4, we read

"Jesus said, 'Truly I say to you,
unless you turn and become like
children, you will never enter the
kingdom of heaven. Whosoever
humbles himself like this child,
he is the greatest in the kingdom
of heaven.'"

Lord, when we look into the face
of our children and realize how
utterly dependent they are on us,
give us wisdom to humble
ourselves before You and beg
You with childlike faith to meet
our needs.

We pray in Your name, Father!

Amen

March 6

Welcome to A One Minute Daily
Scripture and Prayer!

In the 1st chapter of
Deuteronomy, verses 16 - 18,
we read

"At that time Moses instructed
the judges, 'You must hear
the cases of your fellow
Israelites and the foreigners
living among you. Be perfectly
fair in your decisions and
impartial in your judgments. Hear
the cases of those who are poor
as well as those who are rich.
Don't be afraid of anyone's
anger, for the decision you make
is God's decision. Bring me any
cases that are too difficult for
you, and I will handle them.'"

Lord, send us men and women,
like Moses, to be our judges who
will be fair in their judgments for
the poor and the aliens living
among us, so that there will be
real justice for everyone
in our courts and in our land.

We pray in Your name, Lord!

Amen

March 7

Welcome to A One Minute Daily
Scripture and Prayer!

In the 15th chapter of Jeremiah,
verse 16, we read

"When I discovered your word, I
devoured them. They are my joy
and my heart's delight; for I bear
your name, O Lord God of
Heaven's Armies."

Precious Lord, thank You for
giving us Your Word - our Bible.
Help us to read, pray, and digest
every word of it, for in it we find
how You want us to live with
joy and abundant life.

We pray in Your name, Lord, our
constant Provider!

Amen

March 8
Welcome to A One Minute Daily
Scripture and Prayer!

In the 22nd chapter of Proverbs,
verses 24 & 25, we read

"Don't befriend angry people or
associate with hot-tempered
people, or you will learn to be
like them and endanger your
soul."

Precious Lord, help us to
recognize people who are
always angry and easily lose
their temper; give us courage
and wisdom not be their friend.
Give us every grace we need to
follow You and to be led by You
so that when we are tempted to
unrighteous and unholy anger,
we will avoid becoming
consumed by those feelings.

We pray in Your name, Lord of
Peace!

Amen

March 9

Welcome to A One Minute Daily
Scripture and Prayer!

In the 21st chapter of Matthew,
verses 12 & 13, we read

"And Jesus entered the temple
of God and drove out all who
sold and bought in the temple,
and he over-turned the tables of
money-changers and the sects
of those who sold pigeons. He
said to them, 'It is written,
"My house shall be called a
house of prayer" but you
make it a den of robbers.'"

Dear Lord, forgive us when we
grumble that the church is
always wanting us to give
money. Help us to seek church
leaders who are great persons of
prayer who help us to turn our
grumbling into prayer.

We pray in the name of Jesus!

Amen

March 10

Welcome to A One Minute Daily
Scripture and Prayer!

In Psalm 109, verse 31, we read

"For the Lord will stand at the
right hand of the poor and needy
person, to save him from those
who condemn his life."

Lord, open our eyes to see You
standing for the poor and needy
whom You care for and protect.
Help us to love them as You love
them and to do all we can to
protect them from harm.

We pray in Your name, merciful
Lord!

Amen

March 11

Welcome to A One Minute Daily Scripture and Prayer!

In Psalm 127, verse 1, we read

"Unless the Lord builds the house, its laborers labor in vain. Unless the Lord watches over the city, the watchmen stand guard in vain."

Dear Lord, help us to realize that so many of our efforts to build our nation as it needs to be are in vain until we put You in charge, for You alone can build it as it ought to be. Lead us every day to look to You so that we can know what needs to be done.

We pray in Your name, mighty Lord!

Amen

March 12
Welcome to A One Minute Daily
Scripture and Prayer!

In the 4th chapter of Philippians,
verses 6 & 7, we read

"Don't worry about anything;
instead, pray about everything;
tell God your needs and don't
forget to thank Him for His
answers. If you do this, you will
experience God's peace, which
is far more wonderful than the
human mind can understand. His
peace will keep your thoughts
and your hearts quiet and at rest
as you trust in Christ Jesus."

Precious Lord Jesus, thank You
that we can come to You
and tell You all our needs in
prayer, and then experience
Your peace which quiets our
hearts and minds as nothing else
can.

We pray in Your name, Lord of
Peace!

Amen

March 13

Welcome to A One Minute Daily
Scripture and Prayer!

In the 5th chapter of James,
verse 17, we read

"Elias was a man subject to like
passions as we are, and he
prayed earnestly that it might
not rain: and it rained not on the
earth by the space of three years
and six months. And he prayed
again, and the heaven gave rain,
and the earth brought forth fruit."

Dear Lord, give us courage like
Elias to pray earnestly for great
things to happen in our country.
As our prayers are in Your will,
like helping the poor, we can be
confident that You hear us and
answer our prayers.

We pray with thanksgiving that
You answer our prayers!

Amen

March 14
Welcome to A One Minute Daily
Scripture and Prayer!

In the 11th chapter of Mark,
verses 22 - 24, we read

"And Jesus answered them,
'Have faith in God. Truly I say to
you whoever says to this
mountain, be taken up and cast
into the sea, and does not doubt
in his heart, but believes that
what he says will come to pass,
it will be done for him. Therefore
I tell you, whatever you ask in
prayer, believe that you have
received it, and it will be yours.'"

O Lord, I confess that I cannot
always truly believe in my heart
that what I ask for in prayer will
always be done. Forgive me and
give me the kind of faith to ask
and not doubt, so that all my
prayers will be filled with Your
power.

We pray in Your name!

Amen

March 15

Welcome to A One Minute Daily Scripture and Prayer!

In Psalm 51, verses 6 - 8, we read

"Behold you desire truth in the inner being; make me therefore to know wisdom in my innermost heart. Purify me with hyssop, and I shall be clean; wash me and I shall be whiter than snow. Make me hear joy and gladness."

O Lord, forgive us when we go after worldly pleasures and unimportant activities. Give us a desire to seek the wisdom You long to give us, so that our lives will be filled with gladness and joy.

We pray in Your name, wise God!

Amen

March 16

Welcome to A One Minute Daily
Scripture and Prayer!

In the 13th chapter of Hebrews,
verses 7 - 9, we read

"Remember your leaders who
have taught you the Word of
God. Think of all the good that
has come from their lives and try
to trust the Lord as they do.
Jesus Christ is the same
yesterday, today and forever.
So do not be attracted by
strange new ideas. Your spiritual
strength comes as a gift from
God, not from ceremonial rules
about eating certain foods—a
method which, by the way,
hasn't helped those who have
tried it."

Dear Lord, help us to search
until we find men and women
who will teach us Your Word and
live it each day in their lives
so that we can put ourselves into
their care and teaching.

We pray in the name of Jesus,
our Teacher!

Amen

March 17

Welcome to A One Minute Daily
Scripture and Prayer!

In the 15th chapter of Ephesians,
verses 15b & 16, we read

"Jesus took the two groups that
had been opposed to each other
and made them parts of Himself;
thus He fused us together to
become one person, and at last
there was peace. As parts of the
same body, our anger against
each other has disappeared, for
both of us have been reconciled
to God. And so the feud ended
at last at the cross."

O Lord, take away all the
prejudices we have about
other persons and help us to
realize that as Christians
we are all part of Your body and
that You want us to be one.

We pray in the name of Jesus,
Who shed His blood to
make us One!

Amen

March 18
Welcome to A One Minute Daily
Scripture and Prayer!

In the 13th chapter of Hebrews,
verses 15 & 16, we read

"Through Jesus then let us
continually offer up a sacrifice
of praise to God, that is, the fruit
of lips that acknowledge
his name. Do not neglect to do
good and to share what you
have, for such sacrifices are
pleasing to God."

O Lord, give us words that will
speak of the glories of Your
name to each person we
encounter — words that will
magnify Your wondrous works to
all. Let us be known to all as
people who worship You and do
good to others.

We pray in Your name,
wonderful Lord!

Amen

March 19

Welcome to A One Minute Daily
Scripture and Prayer!

In the 2nd chapter of Ephesians,
verses 17 & 18, we read

"And Jesus came and preached
peace to you who were far off
and peace to those who were
near; for through Him we both
have access in one Spirit to the
Father."

Dear Holy Spirit, come to our
churches, our nation and to
the people of the world, in high
places and in low places, and
bring us together to work for
justice so that we will have
peace.

We pray in the holy and saving
name of Jesus, our Lord!

Amen

March 20

Welcome to A One Minute Daily Scripture and Prayer!

In the 8th chapter of Zechariah, verses 22 & 23, we read

"Many peoples and powerful nations will come to Jerusalem to seek the Lord of Heaven's Armies and to ask the Lord of Heaven's Armies for his blessings. In those days ten men from different nations and languages of the world will clutch at the sleeves of one Jew. And they will say, 'Please let us walk with you, for we have heard that God is with you.'"

O Lord, help people of every nation of the world today to see that You love all of us and want us to come together under your banner of Love so that we will have peace in the world.

We pray in Your name, mighty Lord of Peace!

Amen

March 21

Welcome to A One Minute Daily Scripture and Prayer!

In Psalm 146, verses 7 & 8, we read

"The Lord upholds the cause of the oppressed and gives food to the hungry. The Lord sets prisoners free. The Lord gives sight to the blind, the Lord lifts up those who are bowed down, the Lord loves the righteous."

Loving Lord, give us eyes to see how You care for all who are oppressed and held captive. Show us how to be like You by sharing with them our prayers, our presence, our wealth, and by standing with them against all those who are unjust.

We pray in Your name, righteous Lord!

Amen

March 22

Welcome to A One Minute Daily
Scripture and Prayer!

In Psalm 121, verses 6 & 7, we
read

"The sun will not harm you by
day, nor the moon by night. The
Lord will keep you from all harm
—he will watch over your life."

Dear Lord, help us to call out to
You each day when we
encounter any form of
destruction or evil, whether in
nature, or in wicked and angry
people; give us assurance that
You watch over and protect us
and all those we love.

We pray in the name of Jesus,
our strong Protector!

Amen

March 23

Welcome to A One Minute Daily Scripture and Prayer!

In the 21st chapter of Matthew, verses 31b & 32, we read

"Then Jesus explained His meaning: 'Surely evil men and prostitutes will get into the Kingdom before you do. For John the Baptist told you to repent and turn to God, and you wouldn't, while very evil men and prostitutes did. And when you saw this happening you refused to repent so you couldn't believe.'"

Dear Lord, impress on each of us the real need to look into our hearts and see if there are sins, even very small sins or hidden sins, that we need to confess and repent from so that we can believe and be saved.

We pray, Lord Jesus, with gratitude that You forgive and save us!

Amen

March 24

Welcome to A One Minute Daily
Scripture and Prayer!

In the 2nd chapter of Ephesians,
verses 13 & 14, we read

"But now you belong to Christ
Jesus, and though you were far
away from God, now you have
been brought very near to Him
because of what Jesus Christ
has done for you with His blood.
For Christ Himself is our way of
peace. He has made peace
between us Jews and you
Gentiles by making us all one
family breaking down the wall of
contempt that used to separate
us."

O Lord, break down walls
between all peoples and bring
us into Your family. Help us to
reach out to every person of
every race, color, language and
culture; bring us all together
into Your precious family with the
bond of peace that comes from
You.

We pray in Jesus' name!

Amen

March 25

Welcome to A One Minute Daily
Scripture and Prayer!

In the 1st chapter of Matthew,
verse 18, we read

"Now the birth of Jesus the
Messiah took place in this way.
When His mother Mary had been
engaged to Joseph, but before
they lived together, she was
found to be with child from the
Holy Spirit."

Father God, You sent the Holy
Spirit to form Jesus, our Lord
and Savior, in the womb of Mary.
Give us faith to honor Your Spirit
in our bodies.

We pray in Your Holy name!

Amen

March 26
Welcome to A One Minute Daily
Scripture and Prayer!

In Psalm 121, verses 1 & 2, we
read

"I lift up my eyes to the hills —
where does my help come from?
My help comes from the Lord,
the maker of heaven and earth."

Precious Lord, when we hear so
much about people who are
fighting one another and hurting
everyone, help us to lift up our
eyes to You and put all these
problems in Your hands and
realize that You alone are the
Answer and that You alone have
the power to bring peace.

We pray in Your name, Maker of
heaven and earth!

Amen

March 27

Welcome to A One Minute Daily
Scripture and Prayer!

In Psalm 44, verses 6 - 8, we
read

"I do not trust in my bow, my
sword does not bring victory; but
You give us victory over our
enemies, You put our
adversaries to shame. In God we
make our boast all day long, and
we will praise your name
forever."

Mighty Lord, give us wisdom to
see that war and fighting will not
bring us victory but that You give
us protection and victory when
we put our trust in You and
follow your ways.

We pray in Your name, Lord of
victories!

Amen

March 28

Welcome to A One Minute Daily
Scripture and Prayer!

In Psalm 144, verses 7 & 8, we
read

"Reach down from heaven and
rescue me, rescue me from deep
waters, from the power of my
enemies. Their mouths are full of
lies; they swear to tell the truth,
but they lie instead."

Dear Lord, when we are
surrounded by people, even
people in high places who
constantly tell lies, and who are
deceitful in their actions, we cry
out to You to rescue us and to
heal our land.

We pray in Your name, God of
Justice!

Amen

March 29

Welcome to A One Minute Daily Scripture and Prayer!

In the 15th chapter of Matthew, verses 18 – 20, we read

"Jesus said, 'But evil words came from an evil heart and defile the man who says them. For from the heart come evil thoughts, murder, adultery, fornication, theft, lying, and slander. These are what defile; but there is no spiritual defilement from eating without first going through the ritual of ceremonial hand washing.'"

Dear Lord, show us that men and women who speak lies with anger and violence are people with evil hearts and that we should not listen to them. Help us to be careful to use words that are kind and good and honor You.

We pray in Your name, Lord Jesus!

Amen

March 30
Welcome to A One Minute Daily
Scripture and Prayer!

In the 3rd chapter of First John,
verses 17 & 18, we read

"But if someone who is
supposed to be a Christian has
money enough to live well, and
sees a brother in need, and
won't help him—how can God's
love be with him? Little children,
let us stop just saying we love
people, let us really love them,
and show it by our actions."

Dear Lord, forgive us when we
do not share our money with
those in need. Help us to be
generous in our sharing and to
see that love like Yours calls us
to be happy to reach out to those
in need with our prayers,
presence, and wealth.

We pray in the name of Jesus,
Who gave His all!

Amen

March 31

Welcome to A One Minute Daily Scripture and Prayer!

In the 20th chapter of John, verse 29, we read

"Jesus said to Thomas, 'Have you believed because you have seen me? Blessed are those who have not seen and yet have come to believe.'"

Thank You, Risen Lord, that You have given us who have not seen You in the flesh, the blessing of believing in You. Increase our faith so that we can point others to You.

We pray in Your name!

Amen

April 1
Welcome to A One Minute Daily
Scripture and Prayer!

In the 21st chapter of John,
verse 17, we read

"Jesus said to him the third time,
'Simon son of John, do you love
me?' And he said to Jesus,
'Lord, you know everything; you
know that I love you.' Jesus said
to him 'Feed my sheep.'"

Risen Lord Jesus, I want to feed
Your sheep. Show me who the
sheep are whom You want me to
feed, and tell me the best way to
feed them.

We pray in Your name!

Amen

April 2
Welcome to A One Minute Daily
Scripture and Prayer!

In the 21st chapter of John,
verses 13 & 14, we read

"Jesus came and took the bread
and gave it to them and did the
same with the fish. This was
now the third time that Jesus
appeared to the disciples after
he was raised from the dead."

Lord, after Your resurrection You
fed Your disciples by the sea
shore to assure them of Your
love.   When I hunger for Your
Presence and for an assurance
of Your love for me, feed me
through the Scriptures, Holy
Communion, through my
family and by my service to
those in need.

We pray in Your name, Risen
Lord Jesus!

Amen

April 3

Welcome to A One Minute Daily
Scripture and Prayer!

In the 24th chapter of Luke,
verses 48 & 49 , we read

"You are witnesses of these
things. And see, I am sending
upon you what my Father
promised; so stay here in the city
until you have been clothed
with power from on high."

Lord, when I need power to be
Your witness, help me to wait
patiently in Your Presence with
my heart attuned to You. Give
me trust and confidence that You
will send me exactly the power
that I need, at precisely the time
I need it.

We pray in Your name, Lord
Jesus!

Amen

April 4

Welcome to A One Minute Daily
Scripture and Prayer!

In the 1st chapter of First
Corinthians, verses 18 & 19,
we read

"For the word of the cross is folly
to those who are perishing, but
to us who are being saved it is
the power of God.   For it is
written, 'I will destroy the wisdom
of the wise, and the cleverness
of the clever, I will thwart.'"

Precious God, thank You that
You have shown me that the
cross of Christ is the only way I
can be saved. Oh, please move
in Your churches and in all
people to reveal to everyone this
saving truth.

We pray in the name of Jesus,
Who died on the cross for our
salvation!

Amen

April 5
Welcome to A One Minute Daily
Scripture and Prayer!

In the 11th chapter of Luke,
verse 28, we read

"Jesus replied, 'Blessed, rather,
are those who hear the word of
God and obey it.'"

Lord, thank You that I have been
privileged to hear Your Word in
church and in prayer. Help me,
and all who have heard Your
Word, to cherish it in our hearts
and to obey it each day as we
are led.

We pray in Your name, Lord
Jesus!

Amen

April 6
Welcome to A One Minute Daily
Scripture and Prayer!

In the 12th chapter of Luke,
verse 7, we read

"Indeed, the very hairs of your
head are all numbered. Don't be
afraid; you are worth more than
many sparrows."

Lord, when I struggle to believe
that You care about me and my
problems, let me remember
that Jesus says His concern for
me extends even to the hairs on
my head. Let that assurance
give me confidence that
everything about me is important
to You.

We pray in the name of Jesus!

Amen

April 7
Welcome to A One Minute Daily
Scripture and Prayer!

In the 2nd chapter of Ephesians,
verse 8, we read

"By grace are you saved through
faith; and that not of yourself; it is
the gift of God."

Thank You, Lord, that I don't
have to earn my salvation. I
rejoice that all I have to do is to
accept the grace of Your free gift
to me.

We pray in the name of Jesus,
our Saving Lord!

Amen

April 8
Welcome to A One Minute Daily
Scripture and Prayer!

In the 12th chapter of Luke,
verse 8, we read

"I tell you, whoever
acknowledges me before
men, the Son of Man will also
acknowledge him before the
angels of God."

Dear Lord, when I find myself
among people who speak words
that do not honor You, give me
the courage and wisdom to
speak boldly and respectfully of
Your love for me and for all
people.

We pray in Your name, Lord
Jesus!

Amen

April 9
Welcome to A One Minute Daily
Scripture and Prayer!

In the 13th chapter of Luke,
verses 12 &13, we read

"When Jesus saw her, he called
her forward and said to her,
'Woman, you are set free from
your infirmity.' Then he put his
hands on her, and immediately
she straightened up and praised
God."

Merciful Lord, come to all of us
who, today, need Your healing
touch in our bodies, minds,
spirits, and emotions as You did
for the woman who was crippled
in the Bible. Thank You that You
still heal today.

We pray in Your name, Lord
Jesus!

Amen

April 10
Welcome to A One Minute Daily
Scripture and Prayer!

In the 11th chapter of Hebrews,
verse 1, we read

"Faith is the assurance of things
hoped for, the conviction of
things not seen."

Lord, help me to have the
blessed assurance that Your
Word is true and that I can put all
my hope and trust in You.

We pray in the name of Jesus!

Amen

April 11
Welcome to A One Minute Daily
Scripture and Prayer!

In the 14th chapter of John,
verse 6, we read

"Jesus answered, 'I am the way
and the truth and the life.'"

Lord, in the midst of my busy-
ness, when I wonder how to find
peace, give me the wisdom to
turn to You, for You are the
way to peace each day.

We pray in Your name!

Amen

April 12

Welcome to A One Minute Daily
Scripture and Prayer!

In the 10th chapter of
Ecclesiastes, verse 12, we read

"The words of a wise man's
mouth are gracious, and win him
favor, but the lips of a fool will
consume him."

Holy Spirit, give me wisdom that
comes from You so that I will find
favor with You and so bring joy
to all the people I meet and to all
the situations in which I find
myself, especially to my family,
my workplace, and to those who
are hurting.

We pray in the name of Jesus,
our wise Lord!

Amen

April 13
Welcome to A One Minute Daily
Scripture and Prayer!

In the 4th chapter of Matthew,
verse 4, we read

"Man does not live by bread
alone, but by every word that
comes forth from the mouth of
God."

Lord, help me to trust You to
provide for my needs. Let me
live each day listening to You
speak to me and growing in my
trust in Your provision for my life
and for the lives of those I love.

We pray in the name of Jesus!

Amen

April 14
Welcome to A One Minute Daily
Scripture and Prayer!

In the 8th chapter of John, verse
12, we read

"I am the light of the world; the
one who follows me will not walk
in darkness but will have the light
of life."

Dear God, when I am walking in
darkness, let me remember that
Jesus, Your Son, our Savior, is
the true light. Help me to see
His light and to follow Him each
day.

We pray in His blessed name!

Amen

April 15
Welcome to A One Minute Daily
Scripture and Prayer!

In the 11th chapter of Matthew,
verse 25, we read

"I praise you Father, Lord of
heaven and earth, because you
have hidden these things from
the wise and learned and have
revealed them to little children."

Thank You, Lord, that I don't
have to be smart or educated to
know You as my Lord and
Savior. I can just come to You
as a child and You will accept
me as I am with love.

We pray in Your name, Lord
Jesus!

Amen

April 16

Welcome to A One Minute Daily
Scripture and Prayer!

In the 10th chapter of John,
verse 10, we read

"'I have come that they may
have life and have it more
abundantly,' says the Lord."

Teach me, Lord, to live my life in
the ways that You have given so
that I will have an abundant life,
full of joy and meaning.

We pray in Your name, Lord
Jesus!

Amen

April 17

Welcome to A One Minute Daily
Scripture and Prayer!

In Psalm 106, verse 47, we read

"Save us, O Lord our God, and
gather us from the nations, to
give thanks to Your holy name,
and make it our glory to praise
you."

Create, O Lord, in me a strong
desire to praise You; allow me to
recall with joy the many times
You have helped me in my trials.

We pray in the name of Jesus!

Amen

April 18
Welcome to A One Minute Daily
Scripture and Prayer!

We all have needs.

Today you and I can claim the
Lord's promise in the 18th
chapter of Matthew, verse 19,
where Jesus says, "I tell you that
if two of you on earth agree
about anything you ask for, it will
be done for you by my Father in
heaven."

So, I ask you to agree with me
and to speak your own need to
God right now.

(Silently say your need to God.)

Lord, I agree with the person
reading this prayer now, and
together we claim Your promise.

And, we thank You, Lord, that
the need is being met, in the
name of Jesus!

Amen

April 19
Welcome to A One Minute Daily
Scripture and Prayer!

In the 3rd chapter of John, verse
16, we read

"For God so loved the world that
He gave his only Son that
whoever believes in Him should
not perish but have eternal life."

Thank You, Father, for loving us
so much that You gave Jesus,
Your Son, to save us. Help us to
love You, to love ourselves, to
love other people, and to love all
creation as completely as You
love us.

We pray in the name of Jesus!

Amen

April 20

Welcome to A One Minute Daily
Scripture and Prayer!

In Psalm 95, verses 6 & 7, we
read

"O come, let us worship and bow
down, let us kneel before the
Lord our Maker! For He is our
God, and we are the people
of His pasture and the sheep of
His hand."

Mighty God, You have created
us to follow and to praise You.
Give us wisdom to know You are
truly our God, and in knowing
that great fact, help us to
remember every day that our
true happiness comes when we
bow down to worship You.

We pray in the name of Jesus!

Amen

April 21
Welcome to A One Minute Daily
Scripture and Prayer!

In the 12th chapter of Isaiah,
verse 2, we read

"God indeed is my savior, I am
confident and unafraid. My
strength and my courage is the
Lord, and he has been my
savior."

Lord of strength, when I feel so
weak and afraid, give me the
graces I need to put myself in
Your care and to be confident
that You are able to save me
and to know that You want to
protect me.

We pray in the name of Jesus!

Amen

April 22

Welcome to A One Minute Daily
Scripture and Prayer!

In Psalm 84, verse 10, we read

"Better is one day in Your courts
than a thousand elsewhere; I
would rather be a doorkeeper in
the house of my God than dwell
in the tents of the wicked."

Help me, Lord, to live each day
in Your Presence, so that I can
humbly praise You in acts of
mercy, love, compassion, and
justice.

We pray in the name of Jesus,
our humble Lord!

Amen

April 23
Welcome to A One Minute Daily
Scripture and Prayer!

In the 1st chapter of Genesis,
verse 27, we read

"God created man in His own
image, in the image of God He
created him, male and female
He created them."

O Lord God, You created me to
be like You. Give me each day
every grace I need to grow ever
more completely into that image
of who You call me to be.

We pray in the name of Jesus!

Amen

April 24

Welcome to A One Minute Daily
Scripture and Prayer!

In the 2nd chapter of Haggai,
verse 5, we read

"My Spirit remains among you,
just as I promised when you
came out of Egypt. So do not be
afraid."

When fear threatens to
overwhelm us, Lord, help
us to remember and to trust the
promise You made to Your
ancient people through the
prophet, Haggai, that Your Spirit
is always in our midst, and by
that knowledge, calm our fears
today.

We pray with gratitude that Your
Holy Spirit is with us today!

Amen

April 25

Welcome to A One Minute Daily
Scripture and Prayer!

In the 1st chapter of Colossians,
verses 7 & 8, we read

"You learned it from Epaphras
our dear fellow servant who is a
faithful minister of Christ on our
behalf, and who also told us of
your love in the Spirit."

O Lord, give us thankful hearts
as we recall Your faithful
ministers who have taught us
the wonders of Life in You. Bless
them all and help us to be known
to all as people who love You in
the Spirit.

We pray in Your name Loving
Lord!

Amen

April 26

Welcome to A One Minute Daily Scripture and Prayer!

In the 8th chapter of Romans, verses 12 &13, we read

"So then brethren, we are debtors, not to the flesh, to live according to the flesh — for if you live according to the flesh you will die, but if you live by the Spirit, you put to death the deeds of the body and you will live."

Mighty Lord, help me to turn away from seeking to do the things that are only pleasing to my flesh, and to live each day following the Spirit's guidance.

We pray in the name of Jesus!

Amen

April 27

Welcome to A One Minute Daily
Scripture and Prayer!

In Psalm 91, verses 9 & 10, we
read

"Because you have made the
Lord your refuge, the Most High
your habitation, no evil shall
befall you, no scourge come
near your tent."

Lord, thank You that You are
always there for me to run to
when I need You. Help me each
day to rest secure in Your open
arms and to know that You will
always protect me.

We pray in Your name!

Amen

April 28
Welcome to A One Minute Daily
Scripture and Prayer!

In the 4th chapter of First John,
verse 8, we read

"He who does not love does not
know God; for God is love."

Lord, forgive me for the times
when I have not been loving
toward family, friends, strangers
or toward myself. Make me more
loving toward all creation so that
I will be more like You.

We pray in the name of Jesus,
our most loving Lord!

Amen

April 29
Welcome to A One Minute Daily
Scripture and Prayer!

In the 8th chapter of Romans,
verse 28, we read

"We know that in everything God
works for good with those who
love him, who are called
according to his purpose."

Precious Lord, thank You for
assuring me that You are always
with me, even and especially
when things happen that I do not
understand. Deepen my faith
that You are working all these
things out for my good.

We pray in the name of Jesus!

Amen

April 30

Welcome to A One Minute Daily
Scripture and Prayer!

In the 15th chapter of John,
verse 15, we read

"I have called you friends, for all
that I have heard from my Father
I have made known to you."

My heart jumps for joy, Lord, that
You call me Your friend. Thank
You for that privilege. Help me to
look to You daily and learn the
things You want me to know.

We pray in the name of Jesus,
our Divine Friend and brother!

Amen

May 1
Welcome to A One Minute Daily
Scripture and Prayer!

In the 3rd chapter of Acts, verse
19, we read

"Repent therefore, and turn
again, that your sins may be
blotted out, that times of
refreshing may come from the
presence of the Lord."

Holy Spirit, lead each of us to
know the joy of spending time
every day in fellowship with You
in prayer — for as we pray, we
live, here on earth, in Your divine
presence.

We pray in the name of Jesus!

Amen

May 2
Welcome to A One Minute Daily
Scripture and Prayer!

In the 4th chapter of Acts, verse
33, we read

"And with great power the
apostles gave their testimony to
the resurrection of the Lord
Jesus, and great grace was
upon them all."

Lord Jesus, empower, by the
Presence of the Holy Spirit, all of
us who are Your followers to be
courageous witnesses to Your
resurrection from the dead.

We pray in Your name!

Amen

May 3
Welcome to A One Minute Daily
Scripture and Prayer!

In the 5th chapter of Acts, verses
17 & 18, we read

"But the high priest rose up and
all who were with him, that is the
party of the Sadducees, and,
filled with jealousy, they arrested
the apostles and put them in
prison."

Fill us, Lord, with courage and
faith to face all those who seek
to harm us or to make fun of us
because of our belief in You.
Help us to trust Your provision
for us in every situation.

We pray in the name of Jesus!

Amen

May 4
Welcome to A One Minute Daily
Scripture and Prayer!

In the 5th chapter of Acts, verses
20 & 21, we read

"Go and stand in the temple and
speak to the people all the words
of this Life. And when they
heard this they entered the
temple at daybreak and taught"

Lord God, through the power of
the Holy Spirit in us, may we
reach out to teach others the
message of Jesus.

We pray in the name of Our
Triune God!

Amen

May 5
Welcome to A One Minute Daily
Scripture and Prayer!

In Psalm 2, verse 11, we read

"Serve the Lord with fear and
rejoice with trembling."

Lord, thank You that serving You
brings me true happiness.

We pray in the name of Jesus,
Who is our greatest joy!

Amen

May 6

Welcome to A One Minute Daily
Scripture and Prayer!

In the 31st chapter of Jeremiah,
verse 3, we read

"Long ago the Lord said to Israel:
'I have loved you, my people,
with an everlasting love. With
unfailing love I have drawn you
to myself.'"

Dear Lord, draw me to Yourself
as You did long ago with Your
people Israel, for You are the
same today as You were then.
We praise You for Your love that
is everlasting.

We pray in the name of Jesus!

Amen

May 7

Welcome to A One Minute Daily
Scripture and Prayer!

In the 53rd chapter of Isaiah,
verses 2C & 3, we read

"He had no beauty or majesty to
attract us to Him, nothing in His
appearance that we should
desire Him. He was despised
and rejected…a man of sorrows
… and we esteemed Him not."

Lord, Isaiah the prophet
describes You, our Messiah, as
a man possessing no beauty or
majesty. We are ashamed to
admit that we have despised and
rejected, not only You, but also
Your brothers and sisters whose
appearance repels and frightens
us. Forgive us, loving Jesus,
and enable us to offer all Your
children the esteem and dignity
which You have given them.

We pray in Your Name!

Amen

May 8

Welcome to A One Minute Daily
Scripture and Prayer!

In the 5th chapter of Galatians,
verse 24, we read

"And those who belong to Christ
Jesus have crucified the flesh
with its passions and desires."

Lord God, empower me to let go
of all my sinful ways. Help me to
give myself ever more
completely to You, so that You
will control my every thought,
word, and deed.

We pray in the name of Jesus!

Amen

May 9
Welcome to A One Minute Daily
Scripture and Prayer!

In Psalm 30, verse 2, we read

"O Lord my God, I cried to you
for help, and You have healed
me."

Thank You Lord, that when we
are sick and need healing, we
can cry to You, as the Psalmist
did long ago, and You will heal
us, O God Who are the same
today as You were then.

We pray in Your name!

Amen

May 10

Welcome to A One Minute Daily
Scripture and Prayer!

In Psalm 30, verses 2, 9, and 12,
we read

"I cried to you for help: 'What
profit is there in my death?
…You have turned my mourning
into dancing, so my soul may
praise you and not be silent, O
Lord my God, I will give thanks
to you forever.'"

Lord, give us thankful hearts and
give us courage to be bold
witnesses to others of the many
times You have healed and
delivered us from all that could
have injured or killed us.

We pray in the name of Jesus!

Amen

May 11
Welcome to A One Minute Daily
Scripture and Prayer!

In the 1st chapter of Genesis,
verse 2, we read

"And the Spirit of God moved on
the face of the waters."

Lord, open our hearts to see that
from the very beginning of time
Your Holy Spirit has moved in
our world, and that He moves in
our lives today.

We pray in the name of Jesus!

Amen

May 12

Welcome to A One Minute Daily
Scripture and Prayer!

In Psalm 139, verse 7, we read

"Where can I go from Your
Spirit? Or where can I flee
from Your Presence?"

Lord, thank You that Your Holy
Spirit is always in the world and
in my life.   Help me to recognize
and feel Your Presence in this
very moment and in every day.

We pray in the name of Jesus!

Amen

May 13
Welcome to A One Minute Daily
Scripture and Prayer!

In the 22nd chapter of Exodus,
verses 20 – 23, we read

"Whoever sacrifices to any god
other than the Lord must be
destroyed. Do not mistreat an
alien or oppress him for you
were aliens in Egypt. Do not take
advantage of a widow or orphan.
If you do and they cry out to me,
I will certainly hear their cry."

Lord, help us to realize that You
have always taken care of those
who are oppressed - widows,
orphans, and aliens; You have
told us that as Your children You
want us to take care of them too.
Help us to hear Your word and to
be obedient.

We pray in Your name, God of
justice!

Amen

May 14

Welcome to A One Minute Daily
Scripture and Prayer!

In the 3rd chapter of Matthew,
verse 11, we read

"I, John, baptize you with water
for repentance, but one who is
more powerful than I is coming
after me; I am not worthy to carry
his sandals. He will baptize you
with the Holy Spirit and fire."

Lord Jesus, I ask You to baptize
me with the fire of the Holy Spirit,
just as John the Baptist foretold.

We pray in Your holy and
powerful name!

Amen

May 15
Welcome to A One Minute Daily
Scripture and Prayer!

In the 2nd chapter of Acts, verse
38, we read

"Peter said to them, 'Repent, and
be baptized everyone of you in
the name of Jesus Christ so that
your sins may be forgiven, and
so that you will receive the gift of
the Holy Spirit.'"

Thank You, Lord, that when we
are baptized our sins are
forgiven and we receive the Holy
Spirit. Empower us each day to
grow closer to You by the
leading of Your Spirit.

We pray in the name of Jesus!

Amen

May 16

Welcome to A One Minute Daily
Scripture and Prayer!

In at the 1st chapter of Acts,
verse 8, we read

"But you will receive power when
the Holy Spirit has come upon
you; and you will be my
witnesses in Jerusalem, in all
Judea and Samaria, and to the
ends of the earth."

Mighty Lord, thank You that You
have provided for us the power
we need to be Your witnesses,
by sending us Your Holy Spirit.
Show each of us how best to
follow Your Spirit so that we can
witness to Your love, justice, and
peace in the world.

We pray in the name of Jesus!

Amen

May 17
Welcome to A One Minute Daily
Scripture and Prayer!

In the 9th chapter of Acts, verse
31, we read

"Meanwhile the churches
throughout Judea, Galilee, and
Samaria had peace and were
built up. Living in the fear of the
Lord and in the comfort of the
Holy Spirit, it increased in
numbers."

Lord Jesus, open the heart of
Your church, wherever it meets,
to see that it will increase in
numbers, even as the early
churches did, when we live in
peace, and the fear of the Lord,
and the comfort of the Holy
Spirit.

We pray in Your name!

Amen

May 18

Welcome to A One Minute Daily
Scripture and Prayer!

In the 14th chapter of Romans,
verse 17, we read

"For the kingdom of God is not
meat and drink; but
righteousness, and peace, and
joy in the Holy Spirit."

Lord, I want to live a life that is
joyful, peaceful, and righteous,
so fill me with Your Holy Spirit
Who will empower me to live in
ways that bring about these traits
more completely every day.

We pray in the name of Jesus!

Amen

May 19
Welcome to A One Minute Daily
Scripture and Prayer!

In the 43rd chapter of Ezekiel,
verse 2, we read

"There I saw the glory of the God
of Israel coming from the east. I
heard a sound like the roaring of
many waters, and the earth
shone with His glory."

God of Israel, fill my eyes with
visions of Your glory and my
ears with sounds of Your
majesty. Whenever I hear people
say the word "awesome," let my
mind rush to You, Who created
the universe and Whose beloved
Son died for my salvation.

We pray in the holy and precious
Name of Jesus!

Amen

May 20

Welcome to A One Minute Daily Scripture and Prayer!

In the 6th chapter of Deuteronomy, verse 5, we read

"And you shall love the Lord your God with all your heart, and with all your soul and with all your might."

Oh God, help me to obey Your commandment to love You with all my heart, soul, and strength for only in You are we complete and fulfilled.

We pray in the name of Jesus!

Amen

May 21
Welcome to A One Minute Daily
Scripture and Prayer!

In the 8th chapter of Romans,
verse 27, we read

"And he who searches the hearts
of men knows what is the mind
of the Spirit, because the Spirit
intercedes for the saints
according to the will of God."

Precious Holy Spirit, pray for me
because I am not always sure
what the will of God is, but I am
confident in Your prayers on my
behalf because they are always
according to God's will.

We pray in the name of Jesus!

Amen

May 22

Welcome to A One Minute Daily
Scripture and Prayer!

In the 13th chapter of Exodus,
verse 22, we read

"The pillar of cloud by day and
the pillar of fire by night did not
depart from them."

Lord, when we are called on to
go into unknown places, help us
to trust that You will give us
protection as You did for Your
people in the Bible.

We pray in the name of Jesus,
Who is the light of the world.

Amen

May 23
Welcome to A One Minute Daily
Scripture and Prayer!

In the 16th chapter of John,
verse 33, we read

"I have said this to you so that in
me you may have peace. In the
world you face persecution. But
take courage; I have conquered
the world."

Lord, in the midst of turmoil in
the world, help me to grow in my
knowledge of You so that I will
have the peace that only comes
from knowing You.

We pray in Your name, Lord
Jesus Christ!

Amen

May 24

Welcome to A One Minute Daily
Scripture and Prayer!

In the 4th chapter of Philippians,
verse 8, we read

"Finally, beloved, whatsoever is
true, whatsoever is just,
whatsoever is pure, whatsoever
is pleasing, whatsoever is
commendable, if there is any
excellence and if there is
anything worthy of praise,
think about these things."

Precious Lord, help me to think
on the things that are just and
pleasing; rid my mind of all that
is not worthy of Your love.

We pray in Your name, true and
just Lord!

Amen

May 25
Welcome to A One Minute Daily
Scripture and Prayer!

In the 3rd chapter of Philippians,
verse 14, we read

"I press on toward the goal for
the prize of the heavenly call of
God in Christ Jesus."

God of power, when I am hurt by
the trials and tribulations in my
life, give me Your strength, so
that I can press on to receive the
prize which You have promised.

We pray in the name of Christ
Jesus!

Amen

May 26
Welcome to A One Minute Daily
Scripture and Prayer!

In the 6th chapter of Ephesians,
verse 10, we read

"Finally, be strong in the Lord
and in His mighty power."

Mighty Lord Jesus Christ, open
our hearts and eyes to see that
we, who belong to You, have the
power to stand against evil
forces in Your name.

We pray in that name!

Amen

May 27
Welcome to A One Minute Daily
Scripture and Prayer!

In the 6th chapter of Ephesians,
verse 13, we read

"Therefore, put on the full armor
of God, so that when the day of
evil comes, you may be able to
stand your ground, and after you
have done everything, to stand."

Thank You, Lord, for giving us
the graces we need to stand
against evil. When we don't
know how to deal with evil
people, situations or systems,
remind us of Your promise which
we find here, in this chapter of
Ephesians.

We pray in the name of Jesus!

Amen

May 28
Welcome to A One Minute Daily
Scripture and Prayer!

In the 53rd chapter of Isaiah,
verse 6A, we read

"We all, like sheep, have gone
astray, each of us has turned to
his own way."

Thank You, Lord, for Your
wonderful kindness — that
when we insist on having only
our way, when we refuse to
listen to the wisdom and insight
of others, when we are unkind
and judgmental — in all those
times, You continue to love us
and gently to call us back to You!
Thank You, Lord Jesus, for
meeting us exactly where we
are.

We pray in Your Name!

Amen

May 29
Welcome to A One Minute Daily
Scripture and Prayer!

In the 11th chapter of Luke,
verse 13, we read

"If you then, who are evil, know
how to give good gifts to your
children, how much more will the
heavenly Father give the Holy
Spirit to those who ask him."

Heavenly Father, help me realize
that if I ask You to give me the
Holy Spirit, You will — every time
I ask. So now, I ask You, please,
to give me the Holy Spirit.

We pray in the name of Jesus!

Amen

May 30

Welcome to A One Minute Daily Scripture and Prayer!

In the 3rd chapter of Titus, verse 5, we read

"He saved us, not because of any works of righteousness that we have done, but according to his mercy, through the water of rebirth and renewal by the Holy Spirit."

Thank You, Lord, for the gift of baptism through which You save us. Renew each of our days by the power of the Holy Spirit, Who is the gift of salvation in our lives.

We pray in the name of Jesus!

Amen

May 31
Welcome to A One Minute Daily
Scripture and Prayer!

In the 1st chapter of Second
Timothy, verse 7, we read

"For God did not give us a spirit
of cowardice, but rather a spirit
of power and of love and of self-
discipline."

Lord, with the help of the Holy
Spirit, give me power, love and
self-discipline so that I will not
live in fear.

We pray in the name of Jesus!

Amen

June 1

Welcome to A One Minute Daily
Scripture and Prayer!

In the 5th chapter of First
Thessalonians, verse 19, we
read

"Quench not the Spirit."

Open my heart and the heart of
the church wherever it meets
to be a dwelling place where
You, dear Holy Spirit, will be
welcomed, loved, and followed.

We pray in the name of the Lord
Jesus!

Amen

June 2

Welcome to A One Minute Daily Scripture and Prayer!

In the 2nd chapter of Second Thessalonians, verse 13, we read

"But we are bound to give thanks always to God for you, brethren beloved of the Lord, because God hath from the beginning chosen you to salvation through sanctification of the Spirit and belief of the truth."

Lord, give me every day the wisdom to be open in my heart to the work of the Holy Spirit Who cleanses me from my sins, so that I may become more completely holy by Your Presence sanctifying my every thought, word, and action.

We pray in the name of Jesus!

Amen

June 3

Welcome to A One Minute Daily
Scripture and Prayer!

In at the 24th chapter of Luke,
verse 49, we read

"And see, I am sending upon you
what my Father promised, so
stay here in the city until you
have been clothed with power
from on high."

Oh Lord, I need power to be a
better witness to Your love. So,
please fill me each day with Your
Holy Spirit.

We pray in the name of Jesus!

Amen

June 4

Welcome to A One Minute Daily
Scripture and Prayer!

In the 16th chapter of John,
verse 7, we read

"However, I am telling you
nothing but the truth when I say,
it is good for you that I go away.
Because if I do not go away, the
Counsellor will not come to you.
But if I go away, I will send Him
to you to be in close fellowship
with you"

Lord Jesus Christ, thank You
that You have sent the Holy
Spirit to live in our lives to keep
us close to You.

We pray in Your name!

Amen

June 5

Welcome to A One Minute Daily
Scripture and Prayer!

In the 15th chapter of John,
verse 26, we read

"When the Comforter comes
Whom I will send to you from the
Father, the Spirit of Truth Who
comes from the Father, He will
testify regarding me."

Lord, Holy Spirit, come to me
and reveal to me all the things I
need to know about Jesus, so
that I will be a stronger witness
of His love for me and for all
people.

We pray in the name of Jesus!

Amen

June 6

Welcome to A One Minute Daily
Scripture and Prayer!

In the 2nd chapter of First
Corinthians, verses 14 & 15,
we read

"Those who are unspiritual do
not receive the gifts of God's
Spirit, for they are foolishness to
them because they are spiritually
discerned. Those who are
spiritual discern all things."

God of Love, give me spiritual
discernment so that I can receive
the gifts and words of Your Holy
Spirit speaking to me.

We pray in the name of Jesus!

Amen

June 7

Welcome to A One Minute Daily
Scripture and Prayer!

In the 3rd chapter of First
Corinthians, verse 16, we read

"Do you not know that you are
God's temple and that God's
Spirit dwells in you?"

Oh God, when I realize that Your
Holy Spirit lives in me, I feel so
grateful. I also feel a strong
desire to do whatever I can, with
His help, to follow Him daily.

We pray in the name of Jesus!

Amen

June 8
Welcome to A One Minute Daily
Scripture and Prayer!

In the 1st chapter of Second
Timothy, verse 14, we read

"Guard the good treasure
entrusted to you, with the help
of the Holy Spirit living in us."

Lord, help us to be open to Your
Holy Spirit, so that we can guard
all the treasures of life we have
in You.

We pray in the name of Jesus!

Amen

June 9

Welcome to A One Minute Daily
Scripture and Prayer!

In the 3rd chapter of First
Corinthians, verses 19 & 20,
we read

"For the wisdom of this world is
foolishness with God. For it is
written, 'He catches the wise in
their craftiness' and again, 'The
Lord knows the thoughts of the
wise that they are futile.'"

Wise God, You know all things.
Help us to be ever more focused
on You, so that we will receive
guidance from Your Holy Spirit
for the big decisions in our lives
and for the ordinary times as
well.

We pray in the name of Jesus!

Amen

June 10
Welcome to A One Minute Daily
Scripture and Prayer!

In the 12th chapter of First
Corinthians, verse 8, we read

"Now there are varieties of gifts,
but the same Spirit! To each is
given the manifestation of the
Spirit for the common good. To
one is given through the Spirit
the utterance of wisdom."

Lord, Holy Spirit, I need wisdom
each day to make both large and
small decisions in my home,
work, school, and relationships.
Please give me the gift of Your
wisdom.

We pray in the name of Jesus!

Amen

June 11

Welcome to A One Minute Daily
Scripture and Prayer!

In Psalm 67, verses 1 & 2, we
read

"May God be gracious to us and
bless us, that thy way may be
known upon earth, thy saving
power among the nations."

Lord God, send a mighty
outpouring of your Holy Spirit
upon the whole world that people
of all nations will know You, Your
love, and Your power to save.

We pray in the name of Jesus!

Amen

June 12
Welcome to A One Minute Daily
Scripture and Prayer!

In the 42nd chapter of Isaiah,
verse 1, we read

"Here is my servant whom I
uphold, my chosen one in whom
I delight; I will put my Spirit on
him and he will bring justice to
the nations."

Mighty God, You sent Your Son,
Jesus, Who calls us to work with
His Spirit to make the world ever
more just. Give us power so that
we can be channels of His love
and justice wherever we are.

We pray in the name of Jesus!

Amen

June 13

Welcome to A One Minute Daily
Scripture and Prayer!

In Psalm 5, verses 10 & 11, we
read

"Create in me a clean heart, O
God. Renew a loyal spirit within
me. Do not banish me from Your
presence, and do not take your
Holy Spirit from me."

Dear Lord, when we are angry or
resentful towards others, or busy
acquiring 'things', cleanse our
hearts and help us to reach out
to You for the courage to be
loyal to You and Your word.
For in Your presence, with the
Holy Spirit living in us, we will be
able to have a clean heart.

We pray in Your name, Lord of
Power!

Amen

176

June 14
Welcome to A One Minute Daily
Scripture and Prayer!

In Psalm 71, verses 1 - 3, we
read

"In you, O Lord, I have taken
refuge; let me never be put to
shame. Rescue me and deliver
me in Your righteousness; turn
your ear to me and save me. Be
my rock of refuge, to which I can
always go."

Thank You, mighty God, that
You are our refuge and that You
always are there for us when we
call out to You.

We pray in the name of Jesus,
Who is our Rock!

Amen

June 15
Welcome to A One Minute Daily
Scripture and Prayer!

In the 6th chapter of Ephesians,
verse 17, we read

"And take the sword of the Spirit
which is the word of God:
praying always with all prayer
and supplication in the Spirit."

Teach me, Holy Spirit, all I need
to know about the Word of God
so that I will pray in Your will.

We pray in Your name!

Amen

June 16
Welcome to A Daily Prayer for
You!

In the 15th chapter of John,
verses 12 & 13, we read

"This is my commandment that
you love one another as I have
loved you. Greater love has no
man than this, that a man lay
down his life for his friends."

Lord, give me the graces I need
to live each day in self-less ways
so that You can use me to
spread Your love wherever I am.

We pray in Your name, God of
Love!

Amen

June 17
Welcome to A One Minute Daily
Scripture and Prayer!

In the 12th chapter of Mark,
verses 32B & 33, we read

"You are right, Teacher (Jesus);
you have truly said that God is
one, and there is no other but
he; and to love him with all the
heart, and with all
understanding, and with all the
strength, and to love one's
neighbor as oneself, is much
more important than all whole
burnt offerings and sacrifices."

God of love, enter into our minds
and hearts and give us
understanding that You desire
only two things of us: to love
You, our God, above all human
riches and treasures and to love
our neighbor without counting
the cost.

We pray in the name of Jesus,
our Lord!

Amen

June 18
Welcome to A One Minute Daily
Scripture and Prayer!

In at the 11th chapter of Luke,
verse 9, we read

"So I say to you, Ask and keep
on asking and it shall be given to
you: seek and keep on seeking,
and you shall find; knock and
keep on knocking, and the door
shall be opened to you."

Lord, when I feel discouraged in
my prayer, help me to persevere
and to keep on asking, for You
hear our pleas, and You will give
us the things that You know are
best.

We pray in Your name, Lord
Jesus!

Amen

June 19
Welcome to A One Minute Daily
Scripture and Prayer!

In the 8th chapter of Romans,
verse 26, we read

"We do not know how to pray as
we ought, but the Holy Spirit
himself intercedes for us with
sighs too deep for words."

Holy Spirit, I ask You, in humility
and confidence, to pray for me
and all those I love, for I know
that Your prayers are perfect.

We pray in the name of Jesus!

Amen

June 20
Welcome to A One Minute Daily
Scripture and Prayer!

In the 6th chapter of Ephesians,
verse 14, we read

"Stand therefore, hold your
ground having tightened the belt
of truth around your loins, and
having put on the breastplate of
integrity, of moral rectitude and
right standing with God."

Lord, in our daily lives help us to
realize that we have You to give
us the strength we need to live
justly and compassionately, for
You are our hope.

We pray in the name of Jesus,
Who is the Truth!

Amen

June 21
Welcome to A One Minute Daily
Scripture and Prayer!

In the 9th chapter of Jeremiah,
verse 24, we read

"But let him who boasts boast
about this: that he understands
and knows me, that I am the
Lord who exercises kindness,
justice and righteousness on
earth, for in these I delight,
declares the Lord."

Heavenly Father, You are our
God who calls us to be just and
righteous in our words and
actions. Empower us each day
to do these things, and so to
please You.

We pray in the name of Jesus!

Amen

June 22
Welcome to A One Minute Daily
Scripture and Prayer!

In the 13th chapter of First
Corinthians, verses 4 & 5,
we read

"Love is patient and kind; love is
not jealous or boastful; it is not
arrogant or rude. Love does not
insist on its own way; it is not
irritable or resentful."

Lord Jesus, thank You for being
our perfect example of all that
love is. Help us to choose to
follow leaders whose words and
actions reflect Your example of
love for all people.

We pray in Your name!

Amen

June 23

Welcome to A One Minute Daily
Scripture and Prayer!

In the 2nd chapter of Genesis,
verse 7, we read

"Then the Lord God formed man
of the dust from the ground and
breathed into his nostrils the
breath of life, and man became a
living being."

Let me, Lord, grasp the might of
Your power in creating a human
being from dust. Help me to
depend on You and Your mighty
power to meet my every need.

We pray in Your name, Heavenly
Father!

Amen

June 24

Welcome to A One Minute Daily
Scripture and Prayer!

In the 12th chapter of Romans,
verse 1, we read

"I appeal to you therefore,
brethren, by the mercies
of God, to present your bodies
as a living sacrifice, holy and
acceptable to God, which is your
spiritual worship."

Thank You Lord, Jesus, for
giving us Your all. Help us, in
response, to give You our all —
mind, body, and soul.

We pray in Your name!

Amen

June 25
Welcome to A One Minute Daily
Scripture and Prayer!

In Psalm 40, verse 4, we read

"Happy are those who make the
Lord their trust, who do not turn
to the proud, to those who go
astray after false gods."

Heavenly Father, thank You that
You have shown us how to have
a happy life by avoiding
selfishness and all other false
gods.

We pray in Your name, true and
only God!

Amen

June 26

Welcome to A One Minute Daily
Scripture and Prayer!

In the 22nd chapter of Matthew,
verse 39, we read

"You shall love your neighbor as
yourself."

Forgive me, Lord, when I fail to
see the needs of people whom I
do not know and even the needs
of those I do know. Let me see
every person as You see them
and make me want to reach out
to them in my prayer and in my
actions.

We pray in the name of Jesus,
Who is Love!

Amen

June 27

Welcome to A One Minute Daily
Scripture and Prayer!

In the 12th chapter of Romans,
verse 2, we read

"Do not conform any longer to
the pattern of this world, but be
transformed by the renewing of
your mind. Then you will be able
to test and approve what God's
will is— his good and perfect
will."

Dear Lord, I want to know Your
will. Let me see the world, my
family, my neighbors, and
especially to see strangers and
foreigners in the ways You want
me to see them.

We pray in Your name, Lord
Jesus!

Amen

June 28

Welcome to A One Minute Daily
Scripture and Prayer!

In the 11th chapter of Matthew,
verse 25, we read

"At that time Jesus began to say
'I thank You, Father, Lord of
heaven and earth, and
acknowledge openly and joyfully
to Your honor that You have
hidden these things from the
wise and clever and learned, and
have revealed them to babies—
to the childlike, untaught and
unskilled.'"

Lord, thank You that You reveal
to all people, even to those who
are not well educated, and
especially to those who are
simple, the truth that any and all
of us can accept You as our
Savior.

We pray in Your name, precious
and loving Jesus!

Amen

June 29
Welcome to A One Minute Daily
Scripture and Prayer!

In Psalm 84, verses 1 & 2, we
read

"How lovely is your dwelling
place, O Lord of hosts! My soul
longs, indeed it faints for the
courts of the Lord; my heart and
my flesh sing for joy to the living
God."

Divine Lord, give us a hunger for
living in Your Presence, and a
love for worshiping You in places
where You are honored.

We pray in the name of Jesus!

Amen

June 30
Welcome to A One Minute Daily
Scripture and Prayer!

In the 15th chapter of Genesis,
verse 6, we read

"Abram believed the Lord and
He credited it to him as
righteousness."

Lord, when You asked Abram to
follow You to an unknown
destination, he trusted You and
went. When You ask me to
follow You without knowing
where I will end up, give me the
kind of faith that Abram had.

We pray in Your name, Lord of
all provision!

Amen

July 1
Welcome to A One Minute Daily
Scripture and Prayer!

In the 14th chapter of John,
verse 15, we read

"If you love me, you will keep my
commandments."

O Lord, increase my
determination to show my love
for You. Help me to ask You
each day to empower me by the
Holy Spirit to obey Your
commandments.

We pray in the name of Jesus!

Amen

July 2
Welcome to A One Minute Daily
Scripture and Prayer!

In the 5th chapter of Matthew,
verses 34, 35 & 37, we read

"But I say to you, Do not swear
at all, either by heaven, for it is
the throne of God or by earth,
for it is his footstool…. Let what
you say be simply 'Yes' or 'No'
— anything more than this
comes from evil."

Lord, help us to see that our
words are important because
they have power. Allow us to
shape our words and our
conversations according to Your
Word in scripture. When we go
beyond a simple "yes" or "no",
give us wisdom to see that there
is something wrong!

We pray in Your name, Lord
Jesus!

Amen

July 3

Welcome to A One Minute Daily
Scripture and Prayer!

In the 12th chapter of Romans,
verses 4 - 6, we read

"For as in one body we have
many members, and all the
members do not have the same
functions, so we, though many,
are one body in Christ, and
individually members one of
another. Having gifts that differ
according to the grace given to
us; let us use them."

Help us, Lord, to see the value of
each person's gifts in the
community and help us to value
and use the gifts You have given
to each one of us.

We pray in the name of Jesus!

Amen

July 4

Welcome to A One Minute Daily Scripture and Prayer on this American Independence Day as we pray for God's blessings on our country.

In Psalm 85, verse 9, we read

"Surely his salvation is near those who fear him that his glory may dwell in our land."

Lord, let the people of our nation honor You, so that Your kingdom can come in our land.

We pray in the name of Jesus, our King!

Amen

July 5

Welcome to A One Minute Daily
Scripture and Prayer!

In the 22nd chapter of Matthew,
verses 37 & 38, we read

"And Jesus said to him, 'You
shall love the Lord your God
with all your heart, and with all
your soul, and with all your
mind. This is the great and first
commandment.'"

Dear Lord, I want to grow closer
to You. Help me to surrender all
my heart, mind and soul to You,
so that You can have all of me
and be in control of my life. Only
then will I be able to draw ever
more closely to You.

We pray in Your name!

Amen

July 6
Welcome to A One Minute Daily
Scripture and Prayer!

In Psalm 84, verses 11 & 12, we
read

"For the Lord God is a sun and
shield; he bestows favor and
honor. No good thing does the
Lord withhold from those who
walk uprightly. O Lord of hosts,
happy is everyone who trusts in
you."

Holy Spirit, help me to live a holy
life and receive the favor and
honor You offer to those who live
as God tells us to live.

We pray in the name of Jesus!

Amen

July 7
Welcome to A One Minute Daily
Scripture and Prayer!

In the 11th chapter of Hebrews,
verse 26, we read

"Moses regarded disgrace for
the sake of Christ as of greater
value than the treasures of
Egypt, because he was looking
ahead to his reward."

Dear Lord Jesus, give me faith
like Moses who chose to give up
riches and power and position to
respond to God's call and to
follow Your teachings.

We pray in Your name!

Amen

July 8

Welcome to A One Minute Daily
Scripture and Prayer!

In the 11th chapter of Matthew,
verses 28 - 30, we read

"Come to me, all who labor and
are heavy laden, and I will give
you rest. Take my yoke upon
you, and learn from me; for I am
gentle and lowly in heart, and
you will find rest for your souls,
for my yoke is easy and my
burden is light."

Lord, thank You that You invite
us to bring all our worries
to You. We praise You that when
we lay our burdens at Your
feet, You give us rest.

We pray in the name of Jesus!

Amen

July 9
Welcome to A One Minute Daily
Scripture and Prayer!

In the 6th chapter of Ephesians,
verse 18, we read

"Pray at all times in the Spirit
with all prayer and supplication."

Holy Spirit, lead us to pray in
unison with You, for then
our prayer will be in God's will.

We pray in Your name!

Amen

July 10
Welcome to A One Minute Daily
Scripture and Prayer!

In the 11th chapter of Hebrews,
verse 27, we read

"By faith Moses left Egypt, not
fearing the king's anger; he
persevered because he saw Him
who is invisible."

Lord Jesus, help me to
persevere in my faith as
Moses did, even when my trials
seem hard to deal with.

We pray in Your name!

Amen

July 11
Welcome to A One Minute Daily
Scripture and Prayer!

In the 10th chapter of Luke,
verse 2, we read

"And Jesus said to them, 'The
harvest is plentiful, but the
laborers are few; pray, therefore,
the Lord of the harvest to send
out laborers into his harvest.'"

Lord of the harvest, inspire many
to receive you and to accept all
the benefits of peace and joy
that come to us who choose to
become Your followers.

We pray in the name of Jesus!

Amen

July 12
Welcome to A One Minute Daily
Scripture and Prayer!

In Psalm 1, verses 1 & 2, we
read

"Happy are those who do not
follow the advice of the wicked or
take the path that sinners tread,
or sit in the seat of scoffers; but
their delight is in the law of the
Lord, and on his law they
meditate day and night."

Heavenly Father, give us the
graces we need to turn away
from our wrong ways and
thoughts, and help us to keep
our minds and hearts focused on
Your teaching which bring us
true and lasting happiness.

We pray in Your Holy name!

Amen

July 13
Welcome to A One Minute Daily
Scripture and Prayer!

In the 14th chapter of John,
verses 16 & 17, we read

"And Jesus said, 'I will pray the
Father, and he will give you
another counsellor, to be with
you forever, even the Spirit of
truth, whom the world cannot
receive, because it neither sees
him nor knows him; you know
him, for he dwells with you, and
will be with you.'"

Thank You, Lord Jesus Christ,
for praying that I will have the
Holy Spirit living in me. Give all
Your children assurance that
they have the Holy Spirit
living in them as well.

We pray in Your name!

Amen

July 14
Welcome to A One Minute Daily
Scripture and Prayer!

In the 3rd chapter of Ephesians,
verse 16, we read

"That according to the riches of
his glory he may grant you to be
strengthened with might through
his Spirit in the inner man."

Lord, help me each day, by the
indwelling Holy Spirit Who lives
in my heart, to grow stronger in
my love for You and in my
understanding of how very much
You love me.

We pray in Your Holy name!

Amen

July 15
Welcome to A One Minute Daily
Scripture and Prayer!

In the 4th chapter of Ephesians,
verses 2 & 3, we read

"With all lowliness and
meekness, with patience,
forbearing one another in love,
eager to maintain the unity of the
Spirit in the bond of peace."

Holy Spirit, lead each of us to
follow You humbly with true love
for each other so that we can be
united in a community of peace.

We pray in Your Holy name!

Amen

July 16
Welcome to A One Minute Daily
Scripture and Prayer!

In the 15th chapter of Romans,
verse 30, we read

"I appeal to you brethren, by our
Lord Jesus Christ and by the
love of the Spirit, to strive
together with me in your prayers
to God on my behalf."

Heavenly Father, I come to You
in the love of the Spirit and I ask
You to move in Your church and
to bless our pastors and all who
work in the church, drawing them
ever closer to You.

We pray in the name of Jesus!

Amen

July 17
Welcome to A One Minute Daily
Scripture and Prayer!

In the 22nd chapter of Luke,
verse 39, we read

"And Jesus came out, and went
as was his custom to the Mount
of Olives; and when he came to
the place he said to them, 'Pray
that you may not enter into
temptation.'"

Lord Jesus, I pray that You will
help us to follow You, away from
all that tempts us.

We pray in Your powerful and
loving name!

Amen

July 18
Welcome to A One Minute Daily
Scripture and Prayer!

In the 11th chapter of Luke,
verse 36, we read

"Jesus said, 'If then your whole
body is full of light, having no
part dark, it will be wholly bright,
as when a lamp with its rays
gives you light."

Fill me, Lord, with Your Holy
Spirit that He will be the pure
light helping me to shine forth so
that others will see You in me.

We pray in Your name!

Amen

July 19

Welcome to A One Minute Daily Scripture and Prayer!

In the 6th chapter of Ephesians, verse 18, we read

"Pray at all times in the Spirit, with all prayer and supplication. To that end keep alert with all perseverance making supplication for all the saints."

Holy Spirit, lead me to pray as You would have me to pray, every day, many times all through the day, and help me to pray without ceasing for all the saints, not only just for my family, friends and personal needs, but for all Your people everywhere.

We pray in Your Holy name!

Amen

July 20
Welcome to A One Minute Daily
Scripture and Prayer!

In the 5th chapter of Ephesians,
verses 18 & 19, we read

"And do not get drunk with wine,
for that is debauchery; but be
filled with the Spirit, addressing
one another in psalms and
hymns and spiritual songs,
singing and making melody to
the Lord with all your heart."

Lord, fill each of us now with
Your Holy Spirit: We ask Him to
give us a song in our hearts and
that joy which comes only from
having Him alive within us.

We pray in the name of Jesus!

Amen

July 21
Welcome to A One Minute Daily
Scripture and Prayer!

In the 1st chapter of Acts, verse
8, we read

"But you shall receive power
when the Holy Spirit has come
upon you; and you shall be my
witnesses in Jerusalem and in
Judea and Samaria and to the
end of the earth."

Thank You, Lord, that You have
given us the Holy Spirit Who
lives in the hearts of all
believers. We rejoice that He
gives us power to witness to
Your love for us in our homes,
in our towns and to all people.

We pray in the name of Jesus!

Amen

July 22
Welcome to A One Minute Daily
Scripture and Prayer!

In the 2nd chapter of Acts, verse
17, we read

"And in the last days it shall be,
God declares, that I will pour out
my Spirit upon all flesh, and your
sons and your daughters shall
prophesy, and your young men
shall see visions and your old
men shall dream dreams."

Heavenly Father, I ask you to
pour out Your Holy Spirit on men
and women today so that we can
be open to receive the mighty
gift of prophecy which will enable
us to speak Your divine truths.

We pray in the name of Jesus!

Amen

July 23

Welcome to A One Minute Daily
Scripture and Prayer!

In the 14th chapter of John,
verse 12, we read

"Truly truly, I say to you, he who
believes in me will also do the
works that I do; and greater
works than these will he do,
because I go to the Father."

Thank You, Lord, that down
through the ages Your believers
have done mighty miracles.
Inspire each of us to believe that
You will work miracles every day
in our own lives when we ask
with believing, open hearts and
minds.

We pray in the name of Jesus!

Amen

July 24
Welcome to A One Minute Daily
Scripture and Prayer!

In the 4th chapter of Acts, verse
31, we read

"And when they had prayed the
place in which they were
gathered together was shaken;
and they were filled with the Holy
Spirit and spoke the word of God
with boldness."

Lord, unite our hearts and lives
to pray for a mighty outpouring of
Your Holy Spirit in our lives
personally and in the churches.
Empower us to be bold
witnesses for You in our church,
in our families, in our
relationships with others, and in
all the world.

We pray in the name of Jesus!

Amen

July 25

Welcome to A One Minute Daily
Scripture and Prayer!

In the 4th chapter of James,
verses 7 & 8, we read

"Submit therefore to God. Resist
the devil and he will flee from
you. Draw near to God and He
will draw near to you."

Dear God, give us wisdom to
submit to You in our daily lives
so that we can resist the devil
who tries to draw us away from
You. Protect us and all we love
from the evil plans of the devil.

We pray in Your name, God of
Love and Power!

Amen

July 26
Welcome to A One Minute Daily
Scripture and Prayer!

In the 5th chapter of Acts, verse
32, we read

"And we are witnesses to these
things and so is the Holy Spirit
whom God has given to those
who obey him."

Precious Lord, I ask You to give
me every grace I need to obey
You in my life each day, in my
thoughts, words and actions. By
the power and Presence of Your
Holy Spirit living in me, guide me
through each day.

We pray in the name of Jesus!

Amen

July 27
Welcome to A One Minute Daily
Scripture and Prayer!

In the 22nd chapter Luke, verse
41, we read

"And Jesus withdrew from them
about a stone's throw, and knelt
down and prayed."

Dearest Jesus, give us courage
and determination to follow Your
example to go aside to pray as
You did.

We pray in Your name!

Amen

July 28
Welcome to A One Minute Daily
Scripture and Prayer!

In the 11th chapter of Hebrews,
verse 29, we read

"By faith the people crossed the
Red Sea as if on dry land, but
the Egyptians, when they
attempted to do the same, were
drowned."

Lord, inspire our nation to have a
strong faith like Your people did
when they crossed the red sea;
then in all the trials of our days,
we will trust You to deliver us as
You delivered them.

We pray in the name of Jesus,
our great Deliverer!

Amen

July 29
Welcome to A One Minute Daily
Scripture and Prayer!

In Psalm 51, verse 11, we read

"Create in me a pure heart, O
God, and renew a steadfast spirit
within me. Do not cast me from
Your presence or take Your Holy
Spirit from me."

Heavenly Father, give me
wisdom and prayerfulness to live
daily in Your Presence, listening
to and obeying You so that I will
never wander away from Your
Holy Spirit through selfishness or
sloth.

We pray in Your Holy name!

Amen

July 30
Welcome to A One Minute Daily
Scripture and Prayer!

In the 61st chapter of Isaiah,
verse 8, we read

"For I, the Lord, love justice; I
hate robbery and iniquity. In my
faithfulness I will reward them
and make an everlasting
covenant with them."

Heavenly Father, inspire men
and women today to work for
justice for all who are mistreated
in our world and in our nation, so
that we will be people who show
in our actions the love that You
have given to us.

We praying the name of Jesus!

Amen

July 31
Welcome to A One Minute Daily
Scripture and Prayer!

In the 11th chapter of Luke,
verse 23, we read

"Jesus said, 'He who is not with
me is against me, and he who
does not gather with me
scatters.'"

Dear Lord Jesus, give me the
graces I need to choose each
day to be Your helper in all the
things that You call me to do.

We pray in Your name!

Amen

August 1
Welcome to A One Minute Daily
Scripture and Prayer!

In the 3rd chapter of
Ecclesiastes, verse 1, we read

"There is a time for everything
and a season for every activity
under heaven."

Dear Lord, when I get anxious
and get in a hurry about
problems I face, help me to slow
down so that I can take comfort
in Your Word which tells me that
You are with me and that this
season of fear and anxiety will
not last.

We pray in the name of Jesus!

Amen

August 2

Welcome to A One Minute Daily Scripture and Prayer!

In the 11th chapter of Luke, verse 39, we read

"And the Lord said to him, 'Now you Pharisees cleanse the outside of the cup and the dish, but inside you are full of extortion and wickedness.'"

Dear Lord Jesus, thank You that Your blood has cleansed us; help me each day to cast out all the temptations that come to me so that I will be able to be a strong witness of Your great love. Transform the hearts and minds of those for whom wickedness and extortion prevent them from living in Your love.

We pray in Your name!

Amen

August 3
Welcome to A One Minute Daily
Scripture and Prayer!

In the 11th chapter of Hebrews,
verse 31, we read

"By faith Rahab the harlot did not
perish with those who were
disobedient because she had
given friendly welcome to spies."

Precious Lord, help me to see
each person as You see them
and not to presume to judge
anyone.

We pray in the name of Jesus!

Amen

August 4
Welcome to A One Minute Daily
Scripture and Prayer!

In Psalm 57, verses 9 & 10, we
read

"I will praise you, O Lord, among
the nations; I will sing of You
among the peoples. For great is
Your love, reaching to the
heavens; your faithfulness
reaches to the skies. Be
exalted, O God, above the
heavens; let your glory be over
all the earth."

Thank You, Lord, for the great
love which You have for all
people.   Show me how to praise
You for all the wonders and love
You have given to me in my life.
Fill my heart and mouth with
songs of praise for Your
everlasting Love.

We pray in Your name!

Amen

August 5
Welcome to A One Minute Daily
Scripture and Prayer!

In the 6th chapter of Matthew,
verse 34, we read

"Therefore, do not be anxious
about tomorrow, for tomorrow
will be anxious for itself. Let the
day's own trouble be sufficient
for the day."

Help us, Lord, to trust You more
every day; let us live with faith
and trust in Your provisions for
each day; free us by Your power
and love from all our worries
about the future.

We pray in the name of Jesus!

Amen

August 6

Welcome to A One Minute Daily
Scripture and Prayer!

In Psalm 84, verse 10, we read

"For a day in Your courts is
better than a thousand
elsewhere. I would rather be a
doorkeeper in the house of my
God than live in the tents of
wickedness."

Heavenly Father, help each of us
to experience the wonder and
joy of living close to You, so that
the enticements of evil will never
ensnare us.

We pray in Your name!

Amen

August 7

Welcome to A One Minute Daily
Scripture and Prayer!

In the 6th chapter of Matthew,
verse 33, we read

"But seek first his kingdom and
his righteousness, and all these
things shall be yours as well."

Lord Jesus Christ, give us all the
graces we need to put You first
in our lives and to live
righteously so that our days will
be truly happy.

We pray in Your name!

Amen

August 8
Welcome to A One Minute Daily
Scripture and Prayer!

In the 3rd chapter of Jonah,
verse 8, we read

"But let man and beast be
covered with sack cloth. Let
everyone call urgently on God.
Let them give up their evil ways
and their violence."

Heavenly Father, move with
might and power in our nation
and help us to give up our evil
ways and violent actions. Teach
us to ask You to be our God as
they did in Nineveh, so long ago.

We pray in the name of Jesus,
the Prince of Peace!

Amen

August 9
Welcome to A One Minute Daily
Scripture and Prayer!

In the 22nd chapter of Luke,
verses 45 & 46, we read

"And when Jesus rose up from
prayer and was come to his
disciples, he found them
sleeping for sorrow. And he said
unto them, 'Why sleep ye? Rise
and pray, lest you enter into
temptation.'"

Loving Lord, forgive us when we
are busy, lazy, or complacent
about praying. Allow us to see
that by praying, we will avoid
being tempted.

We pray in Your holy name, Lord
Jesus!

Amen

August 10
Welcome to A One Minute Daily
Scripture and Prayer!

In the 6th chapter of Matthew,
verses 9 &10, we read

"Pray then like this: Our Father
who art in heaven, Hallowed be
thy name, Thy kingdom come,
Thy will be done on earth as it is
in heaven."

Father in heaven, I pray that
Your kingdom will come
where I live, so that we will have
peace, love, and good will
among all people, as it is in
heaven.

We pray in Your holy name!

Amen

August 11
Welcome to A One Minute Daily
Scripture and Prayer!

In the 19th chapter of Exodus,
verse 6, we read

"You will be for me a kingdom of
priests and a holy nation."

Lord, open our eyes and hearts
to see that we are all called to be
people who worship, serve and
love You. Let us offer sacrifices
of service and compassion, so
that Your kingdom will come in
our lives and in our nation.

We pray in Your holy name!

Amen

August 12

Welcome to A One Minute Daily Scripture and Prayer!

In the 4th chapter of First John, verse 19, we read

"We love because he first loved us."

Father in Heaven when we look at the cross and see Your Son, Jesus, dying a cruel death so that we can be saved, show us that the Love You have for us calls us to offer that same kind of Love to other people.

We pray in Your name, God of Love!

Amen

August 13
Welcome to A One Minute Daily
Scripture and Prayer!

In the 29th chapter of First
Chronicles, verse 11, we read

"Yours, O Lord, is the greatness
and the power and the glory and
the majesty and the splendor, for
everything in heaven and earth
is yours. Yours, O Lord, is the
kingdom; you are exalted as
head over all."

You, O Lord, are the God of all
the earth and in Your kingdom all
people give you praise. We join
every creature under heaven to
offer You our praises.

We pray in Your mighty name!

Amen

August 14
Welcome to A One Minute Daily
Scripture and Prayer!

In Psalm 119, verse 105, we
read

"Thy word is a lamp unto my
feet, and a light unto my path."

Thank You, Lord, that you have
given us Your Word, our
precious Bible, which puts us in
touch with You by helping us to
know what You are saying to us.

We pray in Your all-knowing
name!

Amen

August 15

Welcome to A One Minute Daily
Scripture and Prayer!

In the 1st chapter of Luke, verse
37, we read

"For with God nothing will be
impossible."

Dear Lord, imprint on my heart
the message that the angel
Gabriel spoke to Mary. Help me
to know that even when
everything looks impossible,
nothing is impossible with You.

We pray in Your mighty name!

Amen

August 16
Welcome to A One Minute Daily
Scripture and Prayer!

In the 61st chapter of Isaiah,
verse 1, we read

"The Spirit of the Sovereign Lord
is on me, because the Lord has
anointed me to preach good
news to the poor. He has sent
me to bind up the broken-
hearted, to proclaim freedom for
captives and release from
darkness for prisoners."

Lord Jesus, lead us, as Your
followers, to reach out to the
poor and the broken-hearted;
help us to work to alleviate their
poverty and the causes of their
broken-heartedness, but most of
all, help us to point them to You
so that they will be healed.

We pray in Your name!

Amen

August 17
Welcome to A One Minute Daily
Scripture and Prayer!

In the 11th chapter of Luke,
verse 13, we read

"If you, then, who are evil know
how to give good gifts to your
children, how much more will
the Heavenly Father give the
Holy Spirit to those who ask
him?"

Heavenly Father, I ask You to
give me the wonderful gift of the
Holy Spirit now and every day so
that He will lead me to give You
glory. I rejoice that You give the
Holy Spirit to all who ask You.

We pray in Your Holy name!

Amen

August 18

Welcome to A One Minute Daily Scripture and Prayer!

In the 5th chapter of Galatians, verse 5, we read

"For we, through the Spirit, wait for the hope of righteousness by faith."

Thank You, Lord Jesus Christ, that by Your death on the cross we have hope that, with the help of the Holy Spirit, we can live lives that are pleasing to You.

We pray in Your name!

Amen

August 19
Welcome to A One Minute Daily
Scripture and Prayer!

In the 6th chapter of
Deuteronomy, verses 4 & 5, we
read

"Hear, O Israel: The Lord is our
God, the Lord alone. You shall
love the Lord your God with all
your heart, and with all your soul
and with all your might."

Precious Lord, thank You that
You love me and want me to
love You above all things or
people. Give me every grace I
need truly to love You with my
whole heart, soul and might.

We pray in the name of Jesus!

Amen

August 20

Welcome to A One Minute Daily Scripture and Prayer!

In the 5th chapter of Galatians, verses 13 &14, we read

"For you were called to freedom, brethren; only do not use your freedom as an opportunity for the flesh, but through love be servants of one another. For the whole law is fulfilled in one word. 'You shall love your neighbor as yourself.'"

Thank You, Lord, that You want us to be servants who choose not to live our lives in selfish desires, but to serve others in a spirit of love and respect for every person.

We pray in the name of Jesus!

Amen

August 21
Welcome to A One Minute Daily
Scripture and Prayer!

In the 8th chapter of Nehemiah,
verse 10, we read

"Then he said to them, 'Go your
way; eat the fat and drink sweet
wine and send portions to him
for whom nothing is prepared; for
this day is holy to our Lord, and
do not be grieved for the joy of
the Lord is your strength.'"

Dear Lord, when I feel sad or
lonely help me to remember that
You are my strength and by that
knowledge and promise
transform my sadness into Your
joy.

We pray in Your Holy name!

Amen

August 22

Welcome to A One Minute Daily
Scripture and Prayer!

In the 5th chapter of Galatians,
verse 16, we read

"But I say walk by the Spirit, and
do not gratify the desires of the
flesh."

Holy Spirit, come to me and lead
me each day so that I will obey
You and not be led to do wrong
things.

We pray in Your Holy name!

Amen

August 23

Welcome to A One Minute Daily Scripture and Prayer!

In the 5th chapter of Galatians, verse 22, we read

"The fruit of the Spirit is love"

And

In the 4th chapter of First John, verses 7 & 8, we read

"Beloved, let us love one another; for love is of God, and he who loves is born of God and knows God. He who does not love does not know God; for God is love."

O Lord of Love, open our hearts to see that You call us to love as You love and to love the unlovely, to love people who are mean to us, to love people who are different from us; indeed You command us to love all people.

We pray in the name of our perfect Lord Jesus!

Amen

August 24

Welcome to A One Minute Daily
Scripture and Prayer!

In the 5th chapter of Galatians,
verse 22, we read

"The fruit of the Spirit is joy."

And

In Psalm 21, verse 6, we read

"Surely you have granted him
eternal blessings and made him
glad with Joy in Your Presence."

Lord God, come to all your
children and give each of us the
deep joy of living in Your
Presence as we pray, worship,
read Your Word, and simply wait
before You — for these times
offer us far more contentment
and joy than any other
experiences we can have.

We pray in the name of Jesus,
Who is our Joy!

Amen

248

August 25
Welcome to A One Minute Daily
Scripture and Prayer!

In the 5th chapter of Galatians,
verse 22, we read

"The fruit of the Spirit is peace."

And

In the 16th chapter of John,
verse 33, we read

"I have told you these things so
that in me you may have peace.
In the world you will have
trouble, but take heart for I have
overcome the world."

Holy Spirit, open our hearts and
minds to see that only in Jesus
will we have peace.

We pray in the name of Jesus,
Who is the Prince of Peace!

Amen

August 26

Welcome to A One Minute Daily
Scripture and Prayer!

In the 5th chapter of Galatians,
verse 22, we read

"The fruit of the Spirit is
patience"

And

In the 19th chapter of Proverbs,
verse 11, we read

"A man's wisdom gives him
patience; it is to his glory to
overlook an offence."

Holy Spirit, give us wisdom so
that we can live patiently in our
trials, trusting You to help us
forgive and love those who
offend us.

We pray in Your Holy name!

Amen

August 27

Welcome to A One Minute Daily Scripture and Prayer!

In the 5th chapter of Galatians, verse 22, we read

"The fruit of the Spirit is kindness"

And

In the 2nd chapter of Ephesians, verse 7, we read

"In order that in the coming ages he might show the incomparable riches of his grace, expressed in his kindness to us in Christ Jesus."

Holy Spirit, empower us to live our lives being kind to family, friends, coworkers, and strangers, even as our Father in Heaven has given us the ultimate example of loving kindness in His Son, Jesus.

We pray in Your Powerful name, most Holy Trinity!

Amen

August 28

Welcome to A One Minute Daily Scripture and Prayer!

In the 5th chapter of Galatians, verse 22, we read

"But the fruit of the Spirit is goodness"

And

In the 11th chapter of Matthew, verse 35, we read

"The good man brings good things out of the good stored up in him."

Holy Spirit, lead us each day to store up the good things of loving You and showing compassion for others in our lives so that we will have a storehouse of goodness to draw from throughout our lives, especially in trying and difficult times when we are tempted to anger and resentment.

We pray in Your name, good Lord!

Amen

August 29

Welcome to A One Minute Daily Scripture and Prayer!

In the 5th chapter of Galatians, verse 23, we read

"The fruit of the Spirit is gentleness"

And

In the 4th chapter of Philippians, verse 5, we read

"Let your gentleness be evident to all."

Holy Spirit, thank You that You are near me. Give me a spirit of gentleness toward my loved ones, and especially make me gentle when I deal with people I do not like so that they may see You in me.

We pray in Your Holy name!

Amen

August 30

Welcome to A One Minute Daily Scripture and Prayer!

In the 5th chapter of Galatians, verse 23, we read

"The fruit of the Spirit is self - control."

And

In the 3rd chapter of First Peter, verse 4, we read

"Instead, it should be that of your inner self, the unfading beauty of a gentle and quiet spirit which is of great worth in God's sight."

Holy Spirit, when I am anxious and nervous, calm me in my inner self so that I can act in ways that please You.

We pray in Your name!

Amen

August 31
Welcome to A One Minute Daily
Scripture and Prayer!

In the 5th chapter of Galatians,
verse 25, we read

"If we live by the Spirit, let us
also walk by the Spirit."

Holy Spirit, help me to put You in
charge of my life and to follow
You so that You will produce
sweet fruit that will fill my life with
love, peace and all the joyful
blessings that come from walking
with You.

We pray in Your Holy name!

Amen

September 1
Welcome to A One Minute Daily
Scripture and Prayer!

In the 53rd chapter of Isaiah,
verses 4A & 5B, we read

"Surely He took up our
infirmities..; the punishment that
brought us peace was upon Him,
and by His wounds we are
healed."

Precious Lord, the punishment
that You took on Yourself and
endured so that we can live in
peace helps me to understand
that You know every pain that
we go through and have
experienced the same pains.
You have won for us the healing
that we need. Thank You! Help
us to call out to You when we
need healing that You long to
give us.

We pray in Your name Healing
Lord!

Amen

September 2

Welcome to A One Minute Daily Scripture and Prayer!

In the 3rd chapter of John, verse 16, we read

"For God so loved the world that he gave his only Son, that whoever believes in him should not perish but have eternal life."

And

In the 16th chapter of John, verse 7, we read

"Nevertheless, I tell you the truth; it is to your advantage that I go away, for if I do not go away the Counsellor will not come to you; but if I go, I will send him to you."

Thank You, Father in heaven, that in Your love for us You sent Jesus to save us. Thank You, Lord Jesus, that when You went back to Your Father, You sent us the Holy Spirit to be our Counsellor.

We pray in Your name, Triune God!

Amen

September 3
Welcome to A One Minute Daily
Scripture and Prayer!

In the 16th chapter of John,
verses 8 - 11, we read

"And when the Holy Spirit
comes, he will convince the
world of sin and righteousness
and judgment concerning sin
because they do not believe in
me, concerning righteousness,
because I go to the Father, and
you will see me no more,
concerning judgment because
the ruler of this world is judged."

Holy Spirit, come and help all of
us to accept Jesus as Lord; help
us to believe that Jesus' death
and resurrection are real; and
help us to know that, because of
Jesus, we have victory over the
devil.

We pray in His saving name!

Amen

September 4

Welcome to A One Minute Daily
Scripture and Prayer!

In the 3rd chapter of First
Corinthians, verse 16, we read

"Do you not know that you are
God's temple and that God's
Spirit dwells in you."

And

In the 7th chapter of John, verses
37 - 39, we read

"On the last day of the feast the
great day, Jesus stood up and
proclaimed, 'If any one thirst, let him
come to me and drink. He who
believes in me as the scripture has
said, "out of his heart shall flow
rivers of living water."' Now this he
said about the Spirit which those
who believed in him were to
receive."

Lord, thank You that You have
made our bodies Your temple where
Your Holy Spirit dwells. Allow us to
give Him first place in our hearts so
that He will use us as wells from
which all Your graces will flow forth.

We pray in Your Holy name!

Amen

September 5
Welcome to A One Minute Daily
Scripture and Prayer!

In the 14th chapter of John,
verses 26 & 27, we read

"But the Comforter which is the
Holy Spirit, whom the Father will
send in my name, he shall teach
you all things and bring things to
your remembrance, whatever I
have said to you. Peace I leave
with you, my peace I give to you;
not as the world gives do I give
to you. Let not your hearts be
troubled, neither let them be
afraid."

Thank You, Lord, that we can be
assured that the Holy Spirit living
in us will bring to our minds the
teachings of Jesus in the Bible
when we need it and that we will
have peace as we abide in Him
and His Word.

We pray in the name of Jesus!

 Amen

September 6
Welcome to A One Minute Daily
Scripture and Prayer!

In the 22nd chapter of Luke,
verse 42, we read

"Father, if thou art willing,
remove this cup from me;
nevertheless not my will, but
thine be done."

Lord, when I am faced with
things I do not like and do not
understand, give me faith to ask
You to deliver me from whatever
it is, as Jesus did, but then to
put it in Your hands and say with
Him, "not my will but thine
be done."

We pray in the name of Jesus!

Amen

September 7

Welcome to A One Minute Daily
Scripture and Prayer!

In the 16th chapter of John,
verses 14 & 15, we read

"He will glorify me for He will take
what is mine and declare it to
you. All that the Father has is
mine; therefore, I said that He
will take what is mine and
declare it to you."

Holy Spirit, You know Jesus in
ways that I am not able to know
Him. So I ask You to teach me
each day and open new horizons
to me so that I will be able to
worship, love and serve Him
better.

We pray in His holy name!

Amen

September 8
Welcome to A One Minute Daily
Scripture and Prayer!

In Psalm 51, verse 12, we read

"Restore to me the joy of thy
salvation and uphold me with a
willing spirit."

Thank You, Lord Jesus, for the
great joy that I had when I first
accepted You as my Lord and
Savior. I ask You to lead all who
do not have that Joy to receive
the free gift You offer to
everyone who comes to You.

We pray in Your name, holy and
loving Savior!

Amen

September 9

Welcome to A One Minute Daily
Scripture and Prayer!

In the 2nd chapter of First
Corinthians, verses 9 & 10,
we read

"But as it is written, 'What no eye
has seen, nor ear heard, nor the
heart of man conceived, what
God has prepared for those who
love him' – these things God has
revealed to us through the Spirit.
For the Spirit searches
everything, even the depths of
God."

Holy Spirit, come to us and teach
us the wonderful things that God
is ready to give to us who are
open to receiving Him.

We pray in Your holy name!

Amen

September 10

Welcome to A One Minute Daily Scripture and Prayer!

In the 1st chapter of First Thessalonians, verse 5, we read

"For our gospel came not unto you in word only, but also in power, and in the Holy Spirit, and in much assurance; as you know what manner of men we were among you for your sake."

Lord, send us men and women today who are living examples of their messages and who are filled with the Holy Spirit so that He can use them with great power to help us to believe, to receive, and to live Your saving message of love and forgiveness.

We pray in the name of Jesus!

Amen

September 11
Welcome to A One Minute Daily
Scripture and Prayer!

In the 23rd chapter of Leviticus,
verse 22, we read

"'When you reap the harvest of
your land, do not reap to the very
edges of your field or gather the
gleanings of your harvest. Leave
them for the poor and the alien. I
am the Lord your God,'"

Dear Lord, help us to remember
that Your Word has always
commanded us to take care of
the poor and even those who are
in our midst who are from other
countries. Forgive us when we
support those in authority who
fail to do this and forgive all of us
when we are unloving toward
others.

We pray in the name of our
Loving Lord!

Amen

September 12
Welcome to A One Minute Daily
Scripture and Prayer!

In the 3rd chapter of Philippians,
verse 10, we read

"Now I have given up everything
else; I have found it to be the
only way to really know Christ
and to experience the mighty
power that brought Him back to
life again."

Dear Lord, open my heart to see
that I must give up everything in
this world so that I can give You
my all and experience the mighty
power of the Holy Spirit living in
me.

We pray in Your powerfully
loving name!

Amen

September 13

Welcome to A One Minute Daily
Scripture and Prayer!

In the 11th chapter of Matthew,
verse 25, we read

"At that time Jesus declared, 'I thank
thee, Father, Lord of heaven and
earth, that thou hast hidden these
things from the wise and clever and
have revealed them to babes.'"

And

In the 3rd chapter of First
Corinthians, verse 18 & 19,
we read

"If any man among you thinks that
he is wise in this age, let him
become a fool that he may become
wise. For the wisdom of this world is
folly with God."

Thank You, Lord, that You have
given us the Bible to be our guide
and that you have told us that by
Your Spirit living in us we can
understand the Scriptures. Let us
humble ourselves like children to
beg the Spirit to be our teacher
because He alone can lead us to
understand what You are saying.

We pray in His name!

Amen

September 14
Welcome to A One Minute Daily
Scripture and Prayer!

In Psalm 21, verse 6, we read

"Surely you have granted him
eternal blessings and made him
glad with the joy of Your
Presence."

Come, Precious Lord, to all of us
who are Your children and give
us the deep joy of living in Your
Presence now and eternally.

We pray in the name of Jesus,
Who is our Joy!

Amen

September 15

Welcome to A One Minute Daily
Scripture and Prayer!

In the 5th chapter of Matthew,
verse 16, we read

"Let your light so shine before
men, that they may see your
good works and give glory to
Your Father who is in heaven."

Lord Jesus, show us how You
want us to do our good deeds,
so that You will get the glory;
prevent us from wanting to be
admired for what we do to help
other people, but, rather, free us
from vanity so that we will rejoice
in the knowledge that You are
using us to point others to our
Heavenly Father.

We pray in Your name, Jesus
our Teacher!

Amen

September 16
Welcome to A One Minute Daily
Scripture and Prayer!

In the 22nd chapter of Luke,
verse 43, we read

"And there appeared an angel
unto Jesus from heaven,
strengthening Him."

Heavenly Father, when we are
very stressed and feel helpless,
as many of us feel now with so
many uncertainties in our world,
send Your angels to lift us up
from despair as You did for
Jesus in His agony.

We pray in His saving name!

Amen

September 17
Welcome to A One Minute Daily
Scripture and Prayer!

In the 18th chapter of John,
verse 37, we read

"Pilate asked Jesus, 'So you are
a king?' Jesus answered, 'You
say that I am a king. For this I
was born, and for this I came
into the world to testify to the
truth. Everyone who belongs to
the truth listens to my voice.'"

Lord Jesus, You came into the
world to be our King. Help us to
remember that we belong to You
and that You are our true King.
Allow us to live in Your kingdom,
which is not of this world, so that
we can listen to You and know
the truth.

We pray in Your name, Lord of
truth!

Amen

September 18
Welcome to A One Minute Daily
Scripture and Prayer!

In the 12th chapter of Isaiah,
verses 2 - 4, we read

"Surely God is my salvation; I will
trust, and not be afraid, for the
Lord God is my strength and my
might; he has become my
salvation. With joy you will draw
water from the wells of salvation.
And you will say in that day: Give
thanks so the Lord, call on his
name; make known his deeds
among the nations; proclaim
that his name is exalted."

You, O Lord, are the mighty God
of the whole world. Thank You
that we can put our trust in You
and not be afraid. Help us to
proclaim boldly Your deeds of
protection, love, and salvation to
all people.

We pray in Your saving name!

Amen

September 19
Welcome to A One Minute Daily
Scripture and Prayer!

In Psalm 122, verses 6 & 7, we
read

"Pray for the peace of
Jerusalem! May they prosper
who love you! Peace be within
your walls, and security within
your towers!"

Lord, give us hearts that can
pray for peace in our own
country and in all the world. We
pray, especially, for peace in
Jerusalem. May our prayers for
peace in that holy city contribute
to peace and prosperity in our
own towns.

We pray in Your name!

Amen

September 20

Welcome to A One Minute Daily Scripture and Prayer!

In the 5th chapter of Matthew, verses 43 - 45, we read

"You have heard that it is said, 'You shall love your neighbor and hate your enemy.' But I say to you, Love your enemies and pray for them who persecute you, so that you may be children of your Father in heaven, for he makes his sun rise on the evil and on the good, and sends rain on the righteous and the unrighteous.'"

Heavenly Father, You are so perfect, and I am far from being like You. I ask You, now, to help me follow Your example: Make me love and pray for those I do not like and for those who are mean to me so that I can become more and more, each day, the person You call me to be.

We pray in the name of Jesus, Who is love!

Amen

September 21
Welcome to A One Minute Daily
Scripture and Prayer!

In Psalm 113, verses 2 - 4, we
read

"Blessed be the name of the
Lord from this time on and
forevermore. From the rising of
the sun to its setting may the
name of the Lord be praised.
The Lord is high above all
nations, and his glory above the
heavens."

Fill me, Lord, with praises for all
the many blessings of life that I
have because of Your great love.
Let my life be a witness every
day to Your love for me and my
love for You.

We pray in Your precious name!

Amen

September 22
Welcome to A One Minute Daily
Scripture and Prayer!

In the 5th chapter of Matthew,
verse 16, we read

"In the same way let your light
shine before others, so that they
may see your good works and
give glory to Your Father in
heaven."

Heavenly Father, inspire in each
of us, and especially in those in
authority, the desire to do good
works of love, peace, and justice
for everyone and to give all the
glory to You.

We pray in the name of Jesus!

Amen

September 23
Welcome to A One Minute Daily
Scripture and Prayer!

In the 8th chapter of Romans,
verse 26, we read

"The Spirit helps us in our
weakness; for we do not know
how to pray as we ought, but the
Spirit himself intercedes for us
with sighs too deep for words."

Lord, thank You that, when I am
lost or confused and don't know
how I need to pray, You have
told us to ask the Holy Spirit to
pray for us. Help me to believe
that the Spirit's prayers for me
are perfectly according to Your
will so that I will always feel at
peace placing my unspoken
needs in His care.

We pray in the name of Jesus!

Amen

September 24
Welcome to A One Minute Daily
Scripture and Prayer!

In the 5th chapter of Matthew,
verses 19 - 21, we read

"Do not store up for yourselves
treasures on earth, where moth
and rust consume and where
thieves break in and steal; but
store up for yourselves treasures
in heaven, where neither moth
nor rust consumes and where
thieves do not break in and steal.
For where your treasure is, there
your heart will be also."

Lord, give us wisdom to see that
all the things that seem
important to us, like having
beautiful clothes or a fancy car,
will only last a short time, but to
have a meaningful relationship
with you, a love that centers on
You, cannot be taken away and
will last forever.

We pray in the name of Jesus!

Amen

September 25

Welcome to A One Minute Daily Scripture and Prayer!

In the 3rd chapter of Colossians, verses 15 - 17, we read

"And let the peace of Christ rule in your hearts, to which indeed you were called in the one body. And let the word of Christ dwell in you richly, teach and admonish one another in all wisdom and sing psalms and hymns and spiritual songs with thankfulness in your hearts to God. And whatever you do in word or deed, do everything in the name of the Lord Jesus, giving thanks to God the Father through him."

Thank You, Father God, for giving us Your Son, Jesus, to be our Savior. Put a song in our hearts and a shout of joy to the world that we have a Savior who loves and saves all who come to Him.

We pray in His saving name!

Amen

September 26

Welcome to A One Minute Daily Scripture and Prayer!

In the 8th chapter of Mark, verses 6 - 9, we read

"So Jesus told the crowd to sit down on the ground. Then He took the seven loaves and, having given thanks, he broke them and gave them to his disciples to set before the people—And they had a few small fish and, having blessed them, he commanded that they also should be set before them— They ate and were satisfied. And there were about four thousand people."

Lord Jesus, You set an example of thanking God for our food. Let us take the time and make the effort to be thankful for our food. As You shared Your food with the four thousand, allow us to share with all who are hungry.

We pray in Your name!

Amen

September 27
Welcome to A One Minute Daily
Scripture and Prayer!

In the 13th chapter of First
Corinthians, verse 12, we read

"For now we see in a mirror
dimly, but then face to face. Now
I know in part, then I shall
understand fully, even as I have
been fully understood."

O Lord, how I look forward to the
time when I will see You clearly,
face to face and understand as
You understand. Help me to
persevere and to believe in this
promise.

We pray in Your all-knowing
name!

Amen

September 28

Welcome to A One Minute Daily Scripture and Prayer!

In Psalm 92, verses 1 - 4, we read

"It is good to give thanks to the Lord, to sing praises to your name, O Most High; to declare your steadfast love in the morning and your faithfulness by night, to the music and the lute and the harp, to the melody of the lyre. For You, O Lord, have made me glad by your work; at the works of your hands I sing for joy."

Precious Lord, how I thank You for the love, faithfulness, mercy, kindnesses and salvation You have given to me and to all who call You their God. Let us shout from the roof tops that You are our Lord and Savior.

We pray in Your mighty name!

Amen

September 29
Welcome to A One Minute Daily
Scripture and Prayer!

In the 5th chapter of Matthew,
verse 24, we read

"No one can serve two masters;
for a slave will either hate the
one and love the other, or be
devoted to the one and despise
the other. You cannot serve
God and wealth."

O Lord, there are so many ways
in our world that entice us to
desire what is gained by wealth.
Give us wisdom, which is a heart
filled with love for You, so that
we will choose to serve and
follow You and Your ways that
bring eternal wealth.

We pray in the name of Jesus,
Who became poor for our
salvation!

Amen

September 30

Welcome to A One Minute Daily Scripture and Prayer!

In the 4th chapter of First John, verse 21, we read

"And this commandment we have from him, that he who loves God should love his brother also."

Dear Lord, it is so easy to love You because You love me so much, but it is not so easy at times to love others. Help me to see every person as You see them, so that I can love them as You love them

We pray in the name of Jesus, Who is love!

Amen

October 1
Welcome to A One Minute Daily
Scripture and Prayer!

In the 1st chapter of First John,
verses 8 & 9, we read

"If we say we have no sin, we
deceive ourselves, and the truth
is not in us. If we confess our
sins, he is faithful and just, and
will forgive our sins and cleanse
us from all unrighteousness."

Dear Lord, thank You that we
can confess all our sins to You
and be confident that You will
forgive us. Touch our hearts so
that we will live lives that honor
You.

We pray in the name of Jesus,
Who shed his blood so that we
can be forgiven and saved!

Amen

October 2

Welcome to A One Minute Daily
Scripture and Prayer!

In the 3rd chapter of John,
verses 16 - 18, we read

"For God so loved the world that
he gave his only Son, that
whoever believes in him shall not
perish but have eternal life. For
God sent the Son into the world,
not to condemn the world, but
that the world might be saved
through him. He who believes in
him is not condemned; he who
does not believe is condemned
already because he has not
believed in the name of the only
Son of God."

O God of Love, thank You for
sending Your only Son Jesus, to
save us, not to condemn us. We
rejoice that You allow us to
receive His love, forgiveness and
salvation when we put our faith
and trust in Him.

We pray in the name of Jesus,
Who gives us eternal life!

Amen

October 3

Welcome to A One Minute Daily
Scripture and Prayer!

In the 1st chapter of Luke,
verses 11 - 13, we read

"And there appeared to
Zechariah an angel of the Lord—
And he was troubled when he
saw him and fear fell upon him.
'Do not be afraid Zechariah, for
your prayer is heard, and your
wife Elizabeth will bear you a
son, and you shall call his name
John.'"

Lord God of miracles, give me
faith to pray for the miracles that
I need in my life. Help me to see
Your miracle of giving Zechariah
and his wife the gift of a son
when they were too old to have
children, and so let me believe
that miracles can come to me
through Your power and love.

We pray in Your name!

Amen

October 4
Welcome to A One Minute Daily
Scripture and Prayer!

In the 1st chapter of Luke,
verses 19 & 20, we read

"And the angel answered
Zechariah, 'I am Gabriel, who
stand in the presence of God;
and I was sent to speak to you
and to bring you this good news.
And behold, you will be silent
and unable to speak until the day
that these things come to pass,
because you did not believe my
words, which will be fulfilled in
their time.'"

Lord, how I long to have You
send an angel to speak to me.
Open my spiritual eyes and ears
to receive Your words to me in
whatever ways You choose to
send them.

We pray in the name of the Lord,
Who speaks to us in many ways!

Amen

October 5
Welcome to A One Minute Daily
Scripture and Prayer!

In the 4th chapter of Daniel,
verse 3, we read

"How great are his signs, how
mighty his wonders! His kingdom
is an eternal kingdom; his
dominion endures from
generation to generation."

Heavenly Father, thank You that
we are able to be part of Your
kingdom here on earth and that
we have the sure and certain
hope that we will be with You
eternally.

We pray in Your name!

Amen

October 6
Welcome to A One Minute Daily
Scripture and Prayer!

In the 3rd chapter of First Kings,
verses 5 & 9, we read

"At Gibeon the Lord appeared to
Solomon in a dream by night,
and God said, 'Ask what I should
give you'…. And Solomon
replied, 'Give your servant
therefore an understanding mind
to govern your people, able to
discern between good and evil;
for who can govern this your
people."

Mighty Lord, fill our leaders with
the desire to ask You to give
them wisdom, as Solomon did,
so that they can have
understanding minds and
discern between good and evil.

We pray in Your name God,
Who alone have all wisdom and
power!

Amen

October 7
Welcome to A One Minute Daily
Scripture and Prayer!

In the 1st chapter of Luke,
verses 44 & 45, we read

"For behold, when the voice of
your greeting came to my ears,
the babe in my womb leaped for
joy. And blessed is she who
believed that there would be a
fulfillment of what was spoken to
her from the Lord."

Dear Lord, give us wisdom to
believe what You have spoken to
us in the Bible as completely as
Mary believed You when You
spoke to her by the angel
Gabriel.

We pray in Your name!

Amen

October 8

Welcome to A One Minute Daily Scripture and Prayer!

In the 1st chapter of Luke, verses 47 - 53, we read

"My soul magnifies the Lord, and my spirit rejoices in God my Savior, for he has regarded the low estate of his handmaiden. For behold, henceforth all generations will call me blessed; for he who is mighty has done great things for me, and holy is his name. And his mercy is on those who fear him from generation to generation. He has shown strength with his arm, he has scattered the proud in the imagination of their hearts, he has put down the mighty from their thrones, and exalted those of low degree; he has filled the hungry with good things, and the rich he has sent empty away."

Lord, put the song of Mary into our hearts that we may join her, rejoicing as we magnify You.

We pray in Your mighty name!

Amen

October 9

Welcome to A One Minute Daily
Scripture and Prayer!

In the 1st chapter of Luke,
verses 63 & 64, we read

"And Zechariah asked for a
writing tablet and he wrote, 'His
name is John.' And they all
marveled. And immediately his
mouth was opened and his
tongue loosed and he spoke,
blessing God."

Lord, give us eyes to see the
miracles that happen around us
every day and mouths to
proclaim the blessings You pour
out on us daily.

We pray in the name of Jesus,
Who speaks miracles into our
lives!

Amen

October 10
Welcome to A One Minute Daily
Scripture and Prayer!

In the 1st chapter of Luke,
verses 67, 76 & 79, we read

"And John's father Zechariah
was filled with the Holy Spirit and
prophesied saying, 'And you,
child, will be called the prophet
of the Most High; for you will go
before the Lord to prepare his
ways, to give knowledge of
salvation to his people in the
forgiveness of their sins, through
the tender mercies of our God
when the day shall dawn upon
us from on high to give light to
those who sit in darkness and in
the shadow of death, to guide
our feet into the way of peace."

Lord, send us people today like
John the Baptist who will point
us to You, so that we will receive
forgiveness of our sins and the
salvation which comes from You.

We pray in the name of Jesus,
Who brings us peace!

Amen

October 11

Welcome to A One Minute Daily Scripture and Prayer!

In the Psalm 1, verses 1 - 4, we read

"Happy are those who do not follow the advice of the wicked, or take the path that sinners tread, or sit in the seat of scoffers; but their delight is in the law of the Lord and on his law they meditate day and night. They are like trees planted by the streams of water, which yield their fruit in its season and their leaves do not wither. In all they do, they prosper. The wicked are not so, but are like chaff that the wind drives away."

Precious Lord, guide us each day to spend our time and energies to follow You and to dwell on every word that You have given us in the Bible and in worship and prayer.

We pray in Your name!

Amen

October 12
Welcome to A One Minute Daily
Scripture and Prayer!

In the 5th chapter of James,
verses 7 - 9, we read

"Be patient, therefore, brethren,
until the coming of the Lord.
Behold the farmer waits for the
precious fruit of the earth, being
patient over it until it receives the
early and the late rain. You also
be patient. Establish your hearts
for the coming of the Lord is at
hand."

Lord, give us determination to
wait patiently with our hearts
firmly set on You. Come to visit
us each day so that we can live
lives that glorify You and so that
we can be at peace in You.

We pray in the name of Jesus!

Amen

October 13
Welcome to A One Minute Daily
Scripture and Prayer!

In the 3rd chapter of Philippians
verses 20 & 21, we read

"We await a savior, the Lord
Jesus Christ, who will change
our mortal bodies, to conform
with his glorified body."

Precious Lord, there are times
when I feel depressed and would
be glad to have You come to
take me to live with You forever.
But since I do not know when
You will come for me, I ask You
to give me the strength to live in
Your Presence this day and
every day and so, find comfort in
Your love.

We pray in Your holy name!

Amen

October 14
Welcome to A One Minute Daily
Scripture and Prayer!

In the 14th chapter of John,
verse 9, we read

"Jesus said to him, 'Have I been
with you so long, and yet you do
not know me, Philip?'"

Dear Lord, forgive us when we
have known You so long and
have benefited from Your love
and gifts time and again, but still
have not taken time to go aside
and become intimate with You
as a Person. Help us to want to
spend time with You alone so
that we will love You more and
more each day.

We pray in the name of Jesus,
our Friend!

Amen

October 15
Welcome to A One Minute Daily
Scripture and Prayer!

In the 11th chapter of Matthew,
verses 28 - 30, we read

"Come to me, all you that are
weary and are carrying heavy
burdens, and I will give you rest.
Take my yoke upon you and
learn from me; for I am gentle
and humble in heart, and you will
find rest for your souls. For my
yoke is easy, and my burden is
light."

Precious Lord, thank You that
You have come to save us and
to show us how much You love
us. We are so grateful that You
open Your arms and give us help
each day and so we do not have
to carry heavy burdens alone.

We pray in Your name, Lord
Jesus!

Amen

October 16
Welcome to A One Minute Daily
Scripture and Prayer!

In the 3rd chapter of Luke,
verses 4 & 6, we read

"As it is written in the book of the
words of the prophet Isaiah, 'The
voice of one crying out in the
wilderness: Prepare the way of
the Lord, make his paths
straight…and all flesh shall see
the salvation of God.'"

Lord God, guide us each day to
know how You want us to cry out
to all people in our thoughts,
words and lives. Use us to point
those we love and, indeed, all
people to You.

We pray in the name of Jesus,
our Savior!

Amen

October 17
Welcome to A One Minute Daily
Scripture and Prayer!

In the 56th chapter of Isaiah,
verses 6 & 7, we read

"And the foreigners who join
themselves to the Lord, to
minister to him, to love the name
of the Lord, and to be his
servants, all who keep the
sabbath, and do not profane it,
and hold fast my covenant—
these I will bring to my holy
mountain, and make them joyful
in my house or prayer; their
burnt offerings and their
sacrifices will be accepted on my
altar; for my house shall be
called a house of prayer for all
peoples."

Thank You Lord, that You love
and accept all people, foreigners
as well as the elect. You have
told us to welcome all into our
churches and to love them in our
hearts; give us strength and
courage to do Your will.

We pray in the name of Jesus!

Amen

October 18
Welcome to A One Minute Daily
Scripture and Prayer!

In the 7th chapter of Isaiah,
verse 14, we read

"Therefore, the Lord Himself will
give you a sign, 'Behold the
virgin shall conceive and bear a
Son and shall call His name
Immanuel.'"

Lord, increase and strengthen
our faith so that we can believe
Your word to us, as Mary did
when she was told she was to
have a child even though she did
not yet have a husband;
because she believed, she had
the privilege of giving birth to
Jesus.

We pray in Your name, O God!

Amen

October 19
Welcome to A One Minute Daily
Scripture and Prayer!

In the 49th chapter of Isaiah,
verse 13, we read

"Sing for joy, O heavens, and
exult, O earth; break forth, O
mountains, into singing! For the
Lord has comforted his people,
and will have compassion on
his suffering ones."

Lord Jesus, You give comfort to
those who suffer. Help us to
follow Your example and be
loving and compassionate to
those who suffer among our
families, friends and to all who
suffer, for You call us to be Your
Presence to them and to offer
them hope.

We pray in Your loving name,
Lord.

Amen

October 20
Welcome to A One Minute Daily
Scripture and Prayer!

In the 1st chapter of Luke,
verses 78 & 79, we read

"Through the tender mercy of our
God, the day shall dawn upon us
from on high to give light to
those who sit in darkness and in
the shadow of death to guide our
feet in the way of peace."

Lord God, You are the light that
takes away our darkness and
ignorance. Guide us each day to
follow You so that we will have
peace in our lives and be
channels of Your peace in the
world.

We pray in the name of Jesus,
the Prince of Peace!

Amen

October 21
Welcome to A One Minute Daily
Scripture and Prayer!

In the 9th chapter of Isaiah,
verse 6, we read

"For unto us a Child is born, unto
us a Son is given; And the
government will be upon His
shoulder. And His name will be
called, 'Wonderful, Counsellor,
Mighty God, Everlasting Father,
Prince of Peace.'"

Father, Your gift of Jesus, Who
is love, is so great that we can
only say, "thank You!" Imprint in
our hearts the words of Isaiah
who says that He has the
government on His shoulders;
may we love and serve Him,
Whose name is Wonderful,
Counsellor, mighty God,
everlasting Father, Prince of
Peace.

We pray in His majestic name!

Amen

October 22
Welcome to A One Minute Daily
Scripture and Prayer!

In the 13th chapter of Hebrews,
verse 5, we read

"Let your conduct be without
covetousness; be content with
such things as you have. For He
Himself has said, 'I will never
leave you nor forsake you.'"

Faithful God, when I am tempted
to think that some new thing will
bring me happiness, let me claim
Your promise, knowing and
believing with my whole being
that You are with me in every
circumstance.

We pray in the Name of Jesus,
Who never forsakes us.

Amen

October 23
Welcome to A One Minute Daily
Scripture and Prayer!

In Psalm 103, verses 8 & 10, we
read

"The Lord is merciful and
gracious, slow to anger,
and abounding in mercy….
He has not dealt with us
according to our sins, nor
punished us according
to our iniquities."

Gracious God, though we have
sinned when we have been
unkind, judgmental, or lacking in
generosity, we thank You for
Your mercy and for the
forgiveness You give us in Christ
Jesus, our Lord, in Whose holy
name we pray.

Amen

October 24
Welcome to A One Minute Daily
Scripture and Prayer!

In the 30th chapter of
Deuteronomy, verses 11 & 14,
we read

"For this commandment which I
command you today is not too
mysterious for you, nor is it far
off. But the word is very near
you, in your mouth and in your
heart, that you may do it."

Revealing God, thank You for
making our mouths and our
hearts and our minds fit to
receive Your word. Give us
discipline to study, and courage
to do what You command.

We pray in the Name of Jesus,
Who is Your divine Word.

Amen

October 25
Welcome to A One Minute Daily
Scripture and Prayer!

In Psalm 118, verses 22 & 23,
we read

"The stone which the builders
rejected has become the chief
cornerstone. This was the Lord's
doing; it is marvelous in our
eyes."

Divine Builder, help us to believe
that You really do know best
when You choose to fashion our
lives in ways we don't
understand or even like.
Deepen our trust in Your
marvelous power and wisdom.

We pray in the Name of Jesus,
Whom human builders
rejected and crucified!

Amen

October 26
Welcome to A One Minute Daily
Scripture and Prayer!

In the 19th chapter of Exodus,
verse 5, we read

"Now therefore, if you will indeed
obey My voice and keep My
covenant, then you shall be a
special treasure to Me above all
people; for all the earth is Mine."

Thank You, God of the universe,
for loving me so deeply that You
call me "a special treasure to"
You! Help me, and all those You
love, to obey Your voice and to
keep Your covenant in the ways
we worship and in the ways
we treat other people.

We pray in the Name of Jesus,
Your most beloved Son!

Amen

October 27
Welcome to A One Minute Daily
Scripture and Prayer!

In the 2nd chapter of Jonah,
verses 1 & 2, we read

"Then Jonah prayed to the Lord
his God from the belly of the fish,
saying, 'I called to the Lord out of
my distress, and He answered
me; out of the belly of Sheol I
cried, and You heard my voice.'"

Thank You, Lord, that You have
answered when I have called to
You from my own pain, sickness,
fear or despair. I beg You now to
hear the cries of people in
prisons, war zones, or those
suffering because of natural
disasters.

We pray in the Name of Jesus!

Amen

October 28
Welcome to A One Minute Daily
Scripture and Prayer!

In the 1st chapter of James,
verse 19, we read

"Know this, dear brothers and
sisters: everyone should be
quick to hear, slow to speak,
slow to wrath."

Help me, Lord, to be more willing
to listen than to speak, more
willing to forgive than to get mad,
especially with my family.

We pray in the Name of Jesus,
Who always listens to our
prayers.

Amen

October 29
Welcome to A One Minute Daily
Scripture and Prayer!

In the 24th chapter of Joshua,
verse 32, we read

"The bones of Joseph, which the
children of Israel had brought up
out of Egypt, they buried at
Shechem, in the plot of ground
which Jacob had bought."

Lord, make us, who have so
much because of Your kindness,
be willing to help the millions of
persons displaced because of
war and natural disasters.

We pray in the Name of Jesus,
Whose family fled Herod's
persecution by going to another
country.

Amen

October 30
Welcome to A One Minute Daily
Scripture and Prayer!

In Psalm 73, verses 6 & 7, we
read

"Pride serves as the neckless of
the wicked; violence covers them
like a garment; their eyes bulge
with abundance."

Hear our prayer, God of power
and compassion, for those who
think that violence is a solution to
life's challenges. Transform the
hearts of all people, especially
the wicked, so that Your Holy
Spirit can lead us all into a fuller
relationship with You.

We pray in the Name of Jesus!

Amen

October 31
Welcome to A One Minute Daily
Scripture and Prayer!

In the 5th chapter of Second
Corinthians, verse 20, we read

"So we are ambassadors for
Christ, since God is making
His appeal through us."

Gracious God, do not let our fear
or sense of inadequacy or just
plain laziness keep us from
taking up this great responsibility
which You have given us: Let us
speak with holy boldness,
humility, confidence and wisdom
about You to all we encounter.

We pray in the Name of Jesus!

Amen

November 1
Welcome to A One Minute Daily
Scripture and Prayer!

In Psalm 69, verse 30, we read

"I will praise the name of God
with a song and will magnify Him
with thanksgiving."

Thank You, Lord, for the great
love that You have shown me in
every way: for my salvation, for
Your love, for the love of friends
and family, especially for the gift
of people who have prayed for
me and who have helped me
to grow closer to You.

We pray with thanksgiving to
You, our dearest Lord!

Amen

November 2
Welcome to A One Minute Daily
Scripture and Prayer!

In the 15th chapter of Jeremiah,
verse 19, we read

"When I found Your words, I
devoured them; they became my
joy and the happiness of my
heart because I love Your name,
O Lord, God of hosts."

Thank You, God of hosts, for
sending us Your words in the
Bible. Help me, each day, to find
greater joy and deeper
happiness as I pray over and
study Scripture.

We pray in the Name of Jesus!

Amen

November 3
Welcome to A One Minute Daily
Scripture and Prayer!

In the 5th chapter of Hosea,
verse 15, we read

"The Lord said, 'I will return
again to my place till they
acknowledge their offence.
Then they will seek my face; in
their affliction they will earnestly
seek Me.'"

Lord God, we are grateful that,
no matter our offence, we can
seek Your face. Thank You for
the kindness You show us when
we look for You.

We pray the name of Jesus!

Amen

November 4
Welcome to A One Minute Daily
Scripture and Prayer!

In Psalm 24, verses 3 & 4, we
read

"Who shall stand in the Lord's
holy place? The man with clean
hands and pure heart, who
desires not worthless things,
who has not sworn so as to
deceive his neighbors."

Lord God, send leaders,
coaches and teachers who will
be examples for children
everywhere. Lift up role models
for us all who do not desire
worthless things, who do not
deceive, and who have pure
hearts.

We pray in the Name of Jesus,
our true and perfect Example!

Amen

November 5
Welcome to A One Minute Daily
Scripture and Prayer!

In the 32nd chapter of Genesis,
verse 24, we read

"This left Jacob all alone in the
camp and a man came and
wrestled with him until dawn
began to break."

O Lord, there are times when I
feel I have wrestled all night with
issues that disturb me. Help me
to remember that I can win my
battles like Jacob did by
persevering in the fight; let my
trust in Your help constantly
grow stronger.

We pray in the name of Jesus!

Amen

November 6

Welcome to A One Minute Daily
Scripture and Prayer!

In the 4th chapter of Philippians,
verses 6 & 7, we read

"Be anxious for nothing, but in
everything by prayer and
supplication, with thanksgiving,
let your requests be made know
to God; and the peace of God,
which surpasses all
understanding, will guard your
hearts and minds through Christ
Jesus."

Thank You, dear Lord, that when
we are facing problems that
confuse us, we can, in our
prayer, tell You our needs
without fear. We thank You for
hearing us; allow us to trust You,
and help us to know that You
will give us the peace of mind
that we are seeking.

We pray in the name of Jesus,
our sure hope!

Amen

November 7

Welcome to A One Minute Daily Scripture and Prayer!

In the 45th chapter of Genesis, verses 4 & 5, we read

"And Joseph said again, 'I am Joseph, your brother whom you sold into slavery in Egypt. But don't be upset and don't be angry with yourselves for selling me in to this place. It was God who sent me here ahead of you to preserve your lives.'"

All-knowing God, give us wisdom to accept those times when we feel that we are being mistreated, and let us entrust those experiences to Your care. Allow us to look at Joseph who suffered greatly, but who forgave those who did him wrong, and who returned good to them. Let us model our lives on this biblical example of returning good to all who do us wrong.

We pray in Your name!

Amen

November 8
Welcome to A One Minute Daily
Scripture and Prayer!

In the 2nd chapter of First John,
verses 15 - 17, we read

"Do not love the world or the
things in the world. If anyone
loves the world, the love of the
Father is not in him. For all that
is in the world – the lust of the
flesh, the lust of the eyes, and
the pride of life – is not of the
Father but is of the world. And
the world is passing away, and
the lust of it; but he who does the
will of God abides forever."

Precious Lord, lead me to know
and to do Your will; protect me
from those who choose to live
lives in lustful, worldly ways.

We pray, Father, in Your Holy
name!

Amen

November 9
Welcome to A One Minute Daily
Scripture and Prayer!

In the 2nd chapter of Exodus,
verses 23 - 25, we read

"Then the children of Israel
groaned because of the bondage
and they cried out; and their cry
came up to God because of the
bondage. And God looked upon
the children of Israel, and God
acknowledged them."

Dear Lord, thank You that You
listen and hear our cries to You
when we pray.   Let us cry out to
You when our nation is in
trouble, and let us trust You to
help us, even as You heard the
cry of the Israelites when You
delivered them from their
bondage and oppressors!

We pray in Your mighty name,
Father.

Amen

November 10
Welcome to A One Minute Daily
Scripture and Prayer!

In the 6th chapter of Ephesians,
verses 10 & 11, we read

"Finally, be strong in the Lord in
the strength of His might. Put on
the whole armor of God, that you
may be able to stand against the
wiles of the devil."

Thank You, Lord, that we are
able to trust You to be our
strength, for You are mighty and
good. Protect us as we strive to
combat the many tricks the devil
uses to destroy us.

We pray in the mighty name of
Jesus, our strong Lord!

Amen

November 11

Welcome to A One Minute Daily Scripture and Prayer!

In the 26th chapter of Isaiah, verses 1-4, we read

"We have a strong city, the Lord sets up salvation as walls and bulwarks. Open the gates that the righteous nation which keeps her faith and her troth with God may enter in. You will guard him in perfect peace whose mind is stayed on You because he commits himself to You, leans on You, hopes in You. So trust in the Lord, commit yourself to him, hope in Him forever, for the Lord God is an everlasting rock — the Rock of ages."

O Lord, let our nation be righteous; let us put our trust and hope in You; let us commit ourselves to You, the Rock of ages, and in that way, honor those who have given their all to protect us.

We pray in Your mighty name!

Amen

November 12
Welcome to A One Minute Daily
Scripture and Prayer!

In the 6th chapter of Ephesians,
verse 16, we read

"Besides all these, taking the
shield of faith, with which you
can quench all the flaming darts
of the evil one."

Oh Lord, give us faith to be our
strong shield when we encounter
unkind remarks, vicious lies, and
other things that happen in a
world which too often welcomes
the devil's tricks and cruelties!

We pray in the name of Jesus,
our strong Deliverer!

Amen

November 13
Welcome to A One Minute Daily
Scripture and Prayer!

In the 6th chapter of Ephesians,
verse 17, we read

"And take the helmet of salvation
and the sword of the Spirit which
is the word of God."

Thank You, Lord God, that,
because Jesus has died to save
us, we can lean on Him, and on
the Bible which is His Word,
trusting Him to give us all we
need to win our daily battles!

We pray in His Saving name.

Amen

November 14
Welcome to A One Minute Daily
Scripture and Prayer!

In the 6th chapter of Ephesians,
verse 19, we read

"And pray for me, that utterance
may be given me in opening my
mouth boldly to proclaim the
mystery of the gospel."

Oh Lord, I ask You to give me
the right words to explain boldly
and respectfully to my family and
friends and to everyone, that
Jesus came to save every
person, of every race, culture,
and language, because of His
great love for us all.

We pray in His Saving name!

Amen

November 15
Welcome to A One Minute Daily
Scripture and Prayer!

In the 6th chapter of Ephesians,
verse 12, we read

"For we are not contending
against flesh and blood, but
against the principalities, against
the powers, against the world
rulers of this present darkness,
against the spiritual hosts of
wickedness in the heavenly
places."

Oh Lord, as we stand against
evil forces, which You tell us to
do in Scripture, help us to rely on
the weapons You provide for us
in the Bible, in Christian
community, in prayer, faith and
trust in Jesus our Savior which,
by His power and goodness, will
enable us to prevail against all
the powers that might assail us.

We pray with faith in Jesus, our
Savior!

Amen

November 16
Welcome to A One Minute Daily
Scripture and Prayer!

In the 6th chapter of Ephesians,
verse 13, we read

"So use every piece of God's
armor to resist the enemy
whenever he attacks, and when
it is all over, you will still be
standing."

Lord, help us never to forget that
we can stand against the enemy
and not be afraid because You
have given us the weapons we
need to overcome the evil one
when he attacks us.

We pray in the name of Jesus,
our Strong Lord!

Amen

November 17
Welcome to A One Minute Daily
Scripture and Prayer!

In the 3rd chapter of Exodus,
verses 14 & 15, we read

"God replied to Moses, 'I am
Who I am. Say this to the people
of Israel: "I am" has sent me to
You.' God also said to Moses,
'Say this to the people of Israel:
the Lord, the God of your
ancestors — the God of
Abraham, the God of Isaac, and
the God of Jacob — has sent me
to you. This is my eternal name,
forever and thus I am to be
remembered throughout all
generations.'"

Mighty God, send us leaders like
Moses to whom You have
spoken and who have listened to
You. Help us to follow them in
our daily battles.

We pray in Your mighty name!

Amen

November 18

Welcome to A One Minute Daily
Scripture and Prayer!

In the 6th chapter of Daniel,
verse 10, we read

"Now when Daniel learned that
the decree had been published,
he went home to his upstairs
room where the windows opened
toward Jerusalem.   Three times
a day he got down on his knees
and prayed, giving thanks to his
God, just as he had done
before."

Lord, give each of us the wisdom
and faith we need to pray to You
over and over each day, even
when the circumstances we face
seem impossible, as Daniel did
when he was facing death in the
lions' den.

We pray in Your all-powerful
name!

Amen

November 19
Welcome to A One Minute Daily
Scripture and Prayer!

In Psalm 100, verses 3 - 5, we
read

"Know ye that the Lord he is
God: it is he that hath made us,
and not we ourselves: We are
his people and the sheep of his
pasture—Enter into his gates
with thanksgiving and into his
courts with praise: Be thankful
unto Him and bless his name.
For the Lord is good; his mercy
is everlasting; and his truth
endures to all generations."

Mighty God, thank You for the
blessed privilege of being Your
child, a child of the God, Who is
merciful, loving, and kind and
Who endures to all generations.

We pray in Your name which is
the name above all names!

Amen

November 20

Welcome to A One Minute Daily
Scripture and Prayer!

In the 15th chapter of Genesis,
verses 3 - 6, we read

"And Abram said 'You have
given me no children; so a
servant in my household will
be my heir.' Then the word of the
Lord came to him, 'This man will
not be your heir, but a son
coming from your own body will
be your heir.' Abram believed the
Lord, and He credited it to
Abram as righteousness."

Lord God, Abram prayed to You
and You heard his prayer. Give
us courage to call on You in all
our needs, as Abram did. Help
us to believe that You hear us
and answer our prayers!

We pray in Your name, Heavenly
Father!

Amen

November 21
Welcome to A One Minute Daily
Scripture and Prayer!

In the 5th chapter of First John,
verses 11 & 12, we read

"And this is the testimony, that
God gave us eternal life, and this
life is in his Son. He who has
the Son has life; he who has not
the Son of God has not life."

Father in heaven, thank You for
giving us Your Son, Jesus, so
that we can live eternally in Him.
Help all people to accept Jesus
and receive His love and the
promise of eternal life.

We pray in the name of Jesus,
our true life!

Amen

November 22
Welcome to A One Minute Daily
Scripture and Prayer!

In the 1st chapter of Ruth, verse
6, we read

"Naomi arose with her
daughters-in-law, Ruth and
Orpah, that they might return to
her country for she heard that
the Lord had visited His people
by giving them bread."

Thank You, Lord, for giving us
our daily bread. Fill our hearts
with joy and gratitude for the
generosity You lavish upon us.

We pray in the name of Jesus,
Your greatest gift!

Amen

338

November 23

Welcome to A One Minute Daily Scripture and Prayer!

In the 13th chapter of First Corinthians, verses 1 - 3, we read

"If I speak in the tongues of men and of angels but have not love, I am a noisy gong or a clanging cymbal—If I have all faith so as to remove mountains but have not love I am nothing. If I give away all I have, and if I deliver my body to be burned but have not love, I gain nothing."

Precious Jesus, You taught us the real meaning of love as You hung on the cross. Imprint on our hearts how much You love us each time we see a cross; give us determination to follow You and to love other people in the sacrificial way You have shown us.

We pray in Your name, saving Lord!

Amen

November 24

Welcome to A One Minute Daily
Scripture and Prayer!

In the 2nd chapter of Jonah,
verses 1 - 7, we read

"From inside the fish Jonah
prayed to the Lord his God. He
said: 'In my distress I called to
the Lord and he answered me.'
When my life was ebbing away, I
remembered you, Lord, and my
prayer rose to You."

O Lord, when we feel depressed
and everything seems hopeless,
help us to do as Jonah did in the
belly of the fish and to put our
thoughts on You, praying for
Your help!

We pray in the name of the God
Who delivers us!

Amen

November 25
Welcome to A One Minute Daily
Scripture and Prayer!

In the 5th chapter of Matthew,
verses 2 - 9, we read

"And Jesus opened his mouth
and taught them saying: Blessed
are the poor in spirit—Blessed
are those who mourn— Blessed
are the meek—Blessed are
those who hunger and thirst for
righteousness—Blessed are the
merciful—Blessed are the pure
in heart—Blessed are the
peacemakers"

Thank You, Lord Jesus, for
giving us these teachings that
show us how to be truly happy.
We beg You to help us each day
to fashion our lives in the ways
You have outlined, so that we
can find real happiness.

We ask this in Your name, Lord
Jesus!

Amen

November 26
Welcome to A One Minute Daily
Scripture and Prayer!

In Psalm 37, verses 5 & 6, we
read

"Commit your way to the Lord;
trust in Him and He will do this:
He will make your righteousness
shine like the dawn, the justice of
your cause like the noonday
sun."

Lord, lead me each day to put
You in charge of my life and to
rest in full assurance that You
will give me every grace I need
to walk in the right path.

We pray in Your almighty name!

Amen

342

November 27
Welcome to A One Minute Daily
Scripture and Prayer!

In the 1st chapter of Proverbs,
verse 7, we read

"The fear of the Lord is the
beginning of knowledge,
but fools despise wisdom and
discipline."

Lord, give us wisdom to see how
much You love us and to believe
that all of Your ways are for our
good, even when we have to
endure hardships in life; let
them bring us closer to You.

We pray in Your all-knowing
name!

Amen

November 28
Welcome to A One Minute Daily
Scripture and Prayer!

In the 5th chapter of James,
verses 17 & 18, we read

"Elijah was a man of like nature
with ourselves and he prayed
fervently that it might not rain,
and for three years and six
months it did not rain on the
earth. Then he prayed again and
the heaven gave rain, and the
earth brought forth its fruit."

Thank You, Lord, that You have
given us the gift of prayer, even
though we are ordinary people.
You hear our prayer as You
heard Elijah's prayer. Give us
faith to come to You with
confidence that You hear us,
even when we must wait to hear
Your answer.

We pray in Your name, faithful
Lord!

Amen

November 29
Welcome to A One Minute Daily
Scripture and Prayer!

In the 6th chapter of Galatians,
verses 7 & 8, we read

"Do not be deceived; God is not
mocked, for whatever a man
sows, that he will also reap. For
he who sows to his own flesh,
will reap from the flesh
corruption; but he who sows to
the Spirit will from the Spirit reap
eternal life."

Heavenly Father, lead us each
day to choose to put aside our
selfish, self-centered desires and
to follow the Spirit's guidance to
do good works, to care for others
and to be kind and
compassionate toward each
other, so that may we reap
eternal life.

We pray in Your name, loving
God!

Amen

November 30

Welcome to A One Minute Daily Scripture and Prayer!

In the 20th chapter of Job, verse 5, we read

"The exulting of the wicked is short, and the joy of the godless is but for a moment"

Oh Lord, give me wisdom to recognize that the joy of those who do wrong lasts for only a very short time but that the Joy You give is everlasting.

We pray in Your holy name!

Amen

December 1

Welcome to A One Minute Daily
Scripture and Prayer!

In the 4th chapter of Exodus,
verses 10 & 11, we read

"But Moses pleaded with the
Lord, 'O Lord I'm not very good
with words. I never have been—
and now even though you have
spoken to me, I get tongue-tied
and my words get tangled.'
Then the Lord asked Moses,
'Who makes a person's mouth?
Is it not I, the Lord? Now go; I
will be with you as you speak,
and I will instruct you in what to
say.'"

Lord, when we feel that we
cannot do what we are called to
do, help us know that You will be
with us, just as You were with
Moses who felt that he could not
do what You were asking of him;
give us confidence that You will
give us everything we need to
accomplish what You call us to
do.

We pray in Your name!

Amen

December 2

Welcome to A One Minute Daily
Scripture and Prayer!

In the 6th chapter of Matthew,
verse 6, we read

"When you pray, go into your
room and shut the door and pray
to your Father Who is in secret;
and your Father Who sees in
secret will reward you."

Precious Lord, thank You for the
gift of prayer which lifts us up
into Your Presence. Teach us to
go aside to spend time alone,
waiting before You, so that we
will experience the joy and
peace You give as we live close
to You in secret.

We pray in Your name, dearest
God of Love!

Amen

December 3
Welcome to A One Minute Daily
Scripture and Prayer!

In the 21st chapter of John,
verse 7, we read

"That disciple whom Jesus loved
said to Peter, 'It is the Lord.'
When Simon Peter heard that it
was the Lord, he jumped into the
sea."

Lord Jesus, put people who
know You well into our lives.
And give us the wisdom and
humility we need to listen to
them when they point us to You.

We pray in Your name!

Amen

December 4

Welcome to A One Minute Daily Scripture and Prayer!

In the 6th chapter of First Timothy, verse 10, we read

"For the love of money is the root of all evils; it is through this craving that some have wandered away from the faith and pierced their hearts with many pangs."

Lord, lead us to want only You — to love You and to love other people as You call us to do. Help us to avoid temptations that lure and entice us — temptations which revolve around having money and more money — the big house, the big car, the finest clothing.

We pray in the name of Jesus, Who lived among us as a poor man!

Amen

December 5
Welcome to A One Minute Daily
Scripture and Prayer!

In the 26th chapter of Isaiah,
verse 3, we read

"You will keep him in perfect
peace whose mind is stayed on
You, because he trusts in You."

Dear Lord, help us to put aside
all the voices and activities in the
world that distract us; help us to
keep our minds centered on
You, with always-growing faith
that You are in charge of our
lives and that You will give us
perfect peace.

We pray in Your name, God of
power!

Amen

December 6
Welcome to A One Minute Daily
Scripture and Prayer!

In Psalm 117, verses 1 & 2, we
read

"Praise the Lord, all you nations!
Extol him, all you peoples; for
great is his steadfast love toward
us, and the faithfulness of the
Lord endures forever. Praise the
Lord."

O mighty Lord, move among all
the nations and help us to see
that You alone are the answer to
our every need. We praise You,
oh Lord of Love, and we pray in
Your name!

Amen

December 7
Welcome to A One Minute Daily
Scripture and Prayer!

In the 6th chapter of Matthew,
verses 14 & 15, we read

"For if you forgive men their
trespasses your heavenly Father
also will forgive you; but if you do
not forgive men their trespasses,
neither will your Father forgive
your trespasses."

O Lord, help me truly to forgive
any and all who have been
unkind to me, spoken ill of me,
told untruths to me or about me,
for I know that I, too, have
sinned and yet You have
forgiven me. Help me to be like
You, Lord: let me forgive even
buried grudges so that I can
receive more fully Your
forgiveness.

We pray in the name of Jesus,
Who forgave those who
crucified Him!

Amen

December 8
Welcome to A One Minute Daily
Scripture and Prayer!

In the 1st chapter of Luke, verse
38, we read

"And Mary said, 'Behold I am the
handmaiden of the Lord, let it be
to me according to your word.'
And the angel departed from
her."

Precious Lord, give us the
courage to humble ourselves
and give You our all, as Mary did
by accepting the word of the
angel even when she knew it
was dangerous.

We pray in the name of Jesus!

Amen

December 9
Welcome to A One Minute Daily
Scripture and Prayer!

In the 5th chapter of Acts, verse
3, we read

"But Peter said, 'Ananias, why
has Satan filled your heart to lie
to the Holy Spirit and to keep
back part of the proceeds of the
land?'"

Holy Spirit, help us to be totally
honest in our relationship with
God, for You are a holy and
compassionate Lord. Protect us
when Satan tries to lead us to be
deceitful and when we do things
that we hope will not be known.

We pray in Your name!

Amen

December 10
Welcome to A One Minute Daily
Scripture and Prayer!

In the 9th chapter of Matthew,
verse 9, we read

"As Jesus passed on from there,
he saw a man called Matthew
sitting at the tax office; and he
said to him, 'Follow me!' And he
rose and followed him."

Lord, when you called Matthew,
he obeyed you. Help us to hear
Your call to us, especially as You
ask us to be present to those
who are lonely or afraid; give us
the graces we need to obey You
as Matthew did, so that we can
help others.

We pray in Your name, Lord
Jesus!

Amen

December 11
Welcome to A One Minute Daily
Scripture and Prayer!

In Psalm 30, verse 5, we read

"For His anger is but for a
moment, His favor is for life;
weeping may endure for a night,
but joy comes in the morning."

Dear Lord, when I feel sad or
depressed, when I want to cry,
send Your Spirit to me and let
me realize how near You are to
me; increase my faith so that I
will trust that Your favor is
always there for me. Let me
rejoice in Your arms and fill me
with Your joy.

We pray in Your name, God of
comfort!

Amen

357

December 12
Welcome to A One Minute Daily
Scripture and Prayer!

In the 12th chapter of Acts,
verses 12 & 17, we read

"When Peter realized this he
went to the house of Mary, the
mother of John whose other
name was Mark, where many
were gathered together and
were praying…. But motioning to
them Peter described to them
how the Lord had brought him
out of the prison."

Mighty Lord, impress on all of us
the great privilege and power
You have given us when we
PRAY. Keep us diligent in our
prayers, Lord, so that our
prayers will have the kind
of power which freed Peter from
prison.

We pray in the name of Jesus,
Who answers our prayers!

Amen

December 13
Welcome to A One Minute Daily
Scripture and Prayer!

In the 5th chapter of Matthew,
verses 42 - 44 & 48,
we read

"Give to those who ask, and
don't turn away from those
who borrow. There is a saying,
'Love your friends and hate your
enemies.' But I say Love your
enemies! Pray for those who
persecute you….. In that way
you will we be acting as true
sons of your Father in heaven….
You are to be perfect even as
your Father in heaven is perfect."

Heavenly Father, help us to
surrender our will to You and
each day seek to follow Your
perfect example which we can
only do with the help of the Holy
Spirit living in us!

We pray in the name of Jesus!

Amen

December 14
Welcome to A One Minute Daily
Scripture and Prayer!

In the 40th chapter of Isaiah,
verse 31, we read

"But those who wait on the Lord
shall renew their strength; they
shall mount up with wings like
eagles. They shall run and not
be weary, they shall walk and
not faint."

Dear Lord, when we feel that
things do not look good in our
families, in the nation, or in any
way, give us wisdom to bring our
concerns to You and then simply
to wait for You to guide us so
that we can rest in Your
provision for our needs.

We pray in the name of Jesus,
Who always hears us!

Amen

December 15
Welcome to A One Minute Daily
Scripture and Prayer!

In the 6th chapter of Matthew,
verses 3 & 4, we read

"But when you give alms, do not
let your left hand know what your
right hand is doing, so that your
alms may be in secret; and your
Father who sees in secret will
reward you."

Heavenly Father, give each of us
a desire to reach out to others
who are less fortunate than we
are and to share quietly with
them some of our own goods,
having no desire to be
recognized for what we have
done in response to Your
command.

We pray in Your name, generous
God!

Amen

December 16
Welcome to A One Minute Daily
Scripture and Prayer!

In the 31st chapter of Jeremiah,
verse 3, we read

"Long ago the Lord said to Israel:
'I have loved you, my people,
with an everlasting love; with
unfailing love I have drawn you
to myself.'"

Lord, I ask You to draw me, all
those I love and, indeed, all
people everywhere, to
experience Your unfailing love —
the love that is greater than all
other loves.

We pray in the name of Jesus,
Who died on a cross because of
His great love for us!

Amen

December 17
Welcome to A One Minute Daily
Scripture and Prayer!

In the 49th chapter of Isaiah,
verses 5A & 6B, we read

"And now the Lord says – He
Who formed me in the womb to
be his servant.... 'I will also
make you a light to the Gentiles,
that you may bring my salvation
to the ends of the earth.'"

Thank You, Lord, that Your
concern and love reach to
people everywhere. Enable us
who are followers of Jesus, Your
Son and Servant, to be lights of
salvation, compassion and care
to men and women in our own
nation and to people who are
fleeing oppression the world
over.

We pray in the name of Jesus,
Whose birth we await!

Amen

December 18
Welcome to A One Minute Daily
Scripture and Prayer!

In the 1st chapter of Luke, verses
31 & 37 – 38, we read

"You will be with child and give
birth to a son and you are to give
him the name Jesus… For
nothing is impossible with
God…. 'I am the Lord's servant,'
Mary answered, 'May it be done
to me as you have said.' Then
the angel left her."

Lord, give each of us the
courage and will to do whatever
You ask of us, as Mary did, even
when we do not understand it.
Increase our faith to believe that
You can do what seems
impossible.

We pray in Your name, miracle-
working God!

Amen

December 19
Welcome to A One Minute Daily
Scripture and Prayer!

In the 1st chapter of Matthew,
verses 20B & 21, we read

"An angel of the Lord appeared
to Joseph in a dream, saying,
'Joseph, son of David, do not
fear to take Mary your wife, for
that which is conceived in her is
of the Holy Spirit; she will bear a
son, and you shall call his name
Jesus, for he will save his people
from their sins.'"

Dear Lord, give us the faith to
hear You speak to us, as Joseph
did, and to know that it is You
speaking. Forgive us when we
fail to recognize Your voice.
Send the Holy spirit to us so that
He can lead us to know the
message You want us to hear.

We pray in Your name, Holy
God!

Amen

December 20

Welcome to A One Minute Daily
Scripture and Prayer!

In the 2nd chapter of Luke, verses
4 & 5, we read

"And Joseph also went up from
Galilee, from the city of
Nazareth, to Judea, to the city of
David, which is called
Bethlehem, because he was of
the house and lineage of David
to be enrolled with Mary his
betrothed, who was with child."

Lord, thank You for the
examples of courage that Mary
and Joseph give us in fulfilling
their responsibilities even they
were burdened. Help us to face
and fulfill our duties each day
with courage like they had.

We pray in Your name, Lord,
Who always provide for us!

Amen

December 21

Welcome to A One Minute Daily Scripture and Prayer!

In the 1st chapter of John, verses 1, 5, 9 & 14, we read

"In the beginning was the Word and the Word was with God, and the Word was God… The light shines in the darkness, and the darkness has not overcome it… The true light that enlightens every man was coming into the world… And the Word became flesh and dwelt among us, full of grace and truth; we have beheld his glory, glory as of the only Son from the Father."

Son of God, thank You for coming into the world to bring light into our darkness and for letting us see the wonder and glory that point us to You Who are the Truth.

We pray in Your name, Lord Jesus!

Amen

December 22
Welcome to A One Minute Daily
Scripture and Prayer!

In the 2nd chapter of Luke, verses
6 & 7, we read

"And while they were there, the
time came for her to be
delivered. And she gave birth to
her first-born son and wrapped
him in swaddling clothes and laid
him in a manger, because there
was no place for them in the
inn."

O Lord, give us wisdom and
strength to open our hearts and
homes to let You reign in them.
Help us to realize that You came
as a low-born child, like most of
us, so that You can identify with
us. And yet You are our Savior
and King. Glory and praise to
You!

We pray in Your name, Lord
Jesus!

Amen

December 23
Welcome to A One Minute Daily
Scripture and Prayer!

In the 10th chapter of Luke,
verses 41 & 42, we read

"But the Lord answered her,
'Martha, Martha, you are
anxious and troubled about
many things; one thing is
needful, Mary has chosen the
good portion, which shall not be
taken away from her.'"

O Lord, in these busy times
when we are trying to prepare for
Christmas, put Your words to
Martha in our hearts; remind us
that You invite us to go aside
and sit at Your feet to talk and
listen to You.

We pray in Your name, Lord
Jesus Christ, for Whose birth we
are preparing!

Amen

December 24
Welcome to A One Minute Daily
Scripture and Prayer on this
Christmas Eve!

In the 1st chapter of John, verse
14, we read

"And the Word became flesh and
dwelt among us and we beheld
His glory, the glory as of the only
begotten of the Father, full of
grace and truth."

My heart is full and overflowing
with praises for having the
privilege of knowing You as my
Lord and Savior. Thank You for
coming to earth so that we can
receive all the graces that You
give.

We pray in Your Name, long-
awaited Jesus!

Amen

December 25

Welcome to A One Minute Daily Scripture and Prayer on this Christmas Day!

In the 2nd chapter of Luke, verses 9, 13 & 14, we read

"The angel of the Lord appeared to them and the glory of the Lord shone round about them, and they were struck with great fear…. 'Glory to God in the highest and on earth peace to those on whom God's favor rests.' When the angels went away, the shepherds said, 'Let us go to see this thing that…the Lord has made known to us.'"

Newborn Jesus, in the midst of our personal Christmas celebrations, give us the grace of those angels and shepherds by allowing us to praise You, to work for peace and justice on earth, and to share with others all that You have come to earth to make known to us.

We pray in Your glorious name!

Amen

December 26
Welcome to A One Minute Daily
Scripture and Prayer!

In the 2nd chapter of Luke
verses 15B, 16 & 20,
we read

"The shepherds said to one
another, 'Let us go over to
Bethlehem and see this thing
that has happened which the
Lord has made known to us. And
they went with haste, and found
Mary and Joseph, and the babe
lying in a manger. And the
shepherds, returned, glorifying
and praising God for all they had
heard and seen, as it had been
told them."

Dear Lord, open our ears and
hearts to hear You speak to us
as You spoke to the shepherds.
Let us hear Your message to us
and let us respond with haste to
follow You so that we will find
You.

We pray in Your name, Lord!

Amen

372

December 27

Welcome to A One Minute Daily
Scripture and Prayer!

In the 2nd chapter of Matthew,
verses 1, 2, 9B,10 &11, we read

"Now when Jesus was born in
Bethlehem of Judea in the days of
Herod the king, behold, wise men
from the East came to Jerusalem
saying, 'Where is he who has
been born king of the Jews? For
we have seen his star in the East
and have come to worship him....
and lo, the star which they had
seen in the East went before them
till it came to rest over the place
where the child was. When they
saw the star they rejoiced
exceedingly with great joy, and
going into the house they saw the
child with Mary his mother and
they fell down and worshiped
Him."

Lord, help us to be willing to go
whatever distance is necessary
like the wise men so that we can
worship You and give You glory.

We pray in Your name, newborn
King!

Amen

December 28
Welcome to A One Minute Daily
Scripture and Prayer!

In the 11th chapter of Luke,
verses 27 & 28, we read

"As Jesus was saying these
things, a woman in the crowd
called out, 'Blessed is the mother
who gave you birth and nursed
you.' Jesus replied, 'Blessed
rather are those who hear the
word of God and obey it.'"

Precious Lord, open our ears
and hearts to hear You speak to
us in prayer, in the Bible, in Your
anointed messengers and, then,
to receive Your Word into our
lives. Show us how to live in
obedience to You so that our
lives will be blessed. Give us
every grace we need to obey
Your word.

We pray in Your name, Lord
Jesus!

Amen

December 29
Welcome to A One Minute Daily
Scripture and Prayer!

In the 2nd chapter of Matthew,
verses 13B & 14, we read

"An angel of the Lord appeared
to Joseph in a dream and said,
'Rise take the child and his
mother, and flee to Egypt, and
remain there till I tell you; for
Herod is about to search for the
child to destroy him.' And he
rose and took the child and his
mother by night and departed to
Egypt."

Lord, help us to recognize the
angels You send to us to warn
us of danger. Give us the graces
we need to do as Joseph did and
obey when You speak to us.

We pray in the name of Jesus,
our Lord!

Amen

December 30
Welcome to A One Minute Daily
Scripture and Prayer!

In the 2nd chapter of Luke,
verses 25 & 27, we read

"Now there was a man in
Jerusalem called Simeon, who
was righteous and devout. He
was waiting for the consolation
of Israel and the Holy Spirit was
upon him. Moved by the Spirit he
went into the temple courts.
When the parents brought in the
child Jesus to do for him what
the custom of the law required,
Simeon took the child Jesus in
his arms and praised God."

Dear Lord, help us to surrender
ourselves to be led by the Holy
Spirit as Simeon did. With the
Spirit's guidance, allow us to find
You so that our lives will be filled
with Your salvation and peace.

We pray in Your name, Lord
Jesus!

Amen

December 31

Welcome to A One Minute Daily Scripture and Prayer on this New Year's Eve!

In Psalm 98, verses 1 - 3, we read

"Oh sing to the Lord a new song! Sing to the Lord all the earth. Sing to the Lord, bless His name: Proclaim the good news of His salvation from day to day. Declare His glory among the nations, His wonders among all people."

Lord, as the year comes to a close, fill our hearts with gratitude to You for all the blessings that have come to us in this year that is ending, especially for Your ever-present love, counsel, and protections each day. If we count our blessings, as the song says, and name them one by one, we would never finish we are so blessed!

We pray in the name of Jesus!

Amen

378

Prayers for
Special Days
and
Special Needs

for CHRISTMAS

In the first chapter of Luke,
verses 6 & 7, we read:

"Zechariah and Elizabeth were
both righteous before God,
walking in all the commandments
and ordinances of the Lord
blameless. But they had no child
because Elizabeth was barren
and both were advanced in
years."

Lord, we lift up to You all those
who want to be parents to
children but who have none. We
ask You to bless them
abundantly.

We pray in the name of Your
Child, Jesus!

Amen

A One Minute Daily Scripture and Prayer
for CHRISTMAS

In the 2nd chapter of Matthew,
verse 13, we read:

"An angel of the Lord appeared
to Joseph in a dream and said,
'Get up, take the Child and His
mother, and flee to Egypt and
remain there until I tell you for
Herod is about to search for the
Child to destroy Him."

Lord, in the Bible, we see Jesus
having to flee from His homeland
to another country because King
Herod wanted to kill Him. Bless
and protect all those who are
seeking safety from oppression.

We pray in the Name of Jesus,
Who was Himself welcomed in a
foreign land!

Amen

for CHRISTMAS

In the 2nd chapter of Luke,
verses 4 – 7, we read

"And Joseph also went to Judea,
to the city of David, which is
called Bethlehem, because he
was of the house and lineage of
David to be enrolled with Mary
his betrothed, who was with
child. And while they were there,
the time came for her to be
delivered. And she gave birth to
her first-born son and wrapped
him in swaddling clothes, and
laid him in a manger because
there was no place for them in
the inn."

O Lord, give us the graces we
need always to make
room in our lives, hearts, and
homes for You to be
welcomed and loved.

We pray in Your name!

Amen

A One Minute Daily Scripture and Prayer
for CHRISTMAS

In the 2nd chapter of Luke,
verses 8-14 we read

"And in that region there were
shepherds out in the field ….
And an angel of the Lord
appeared to them, and the glory
the Lord shone around them and
they were filled with fear. And
the angel said to them, 'Be not
afraid; for behold I bring you
good news of great joy which will
come to all people, for to you is
born this day in the city of David
a Savior, who is Christ the Lord.'
… And suddenly there was with
the angel a multitude of the
heavenly host praising God and
saying… 'Glory to God in the
highest and on earth peace
among those with whom he is
pleased!'"

Lord, help us to please You and
join the angels praising You, as
we say, "Glory to God and peace
to His people."

We pray in the name of Jesus!

Amen

for CHRISTMAS

In the 2nd chapter of Matthew, verses 1 & 2, we read

"Now after Jesus was born in Bethlehem of Judea in the days of Herod the king, behold, wise men from the East came to Jerusalem saying, 'Where is He who has been born King of the Jews? For we have seen His star in the East and have come to worship Him.'"

Lord, give us wisdom to follow You even as the wise men of old who came from far away to worship You.

We pray in the name of Jesus, the new born King!

Amen

384

A One Minute Daily Scripture and Prayer
for CHRISTMAS

In the 2nd chapter of Matthew,
verses 9 & 10, we read

"The star which they had seen in
the East went before them, till it
came and stood over where the
young child was. When they saw
the star, they rejoiced with
exceedingly great joy."

Lord, give us hearts that rejoice
when we are led by experiences
that bring us close to where You
are, as the wise men greatly
rejoiced when they saw the star
that had led them to find You.

We pray in the name of Jesus,
Who gives us Joy!

Amen

for CHRISTMAS

In the 2nd chapter of Matthew, verses 11 & 12, we read

"And when they had come into the house, they saw the young child with Mary His mother, and fell down and worshiped Him. And when they had opened their treasures, they presented gifts to Him: gold, frankincense, and myrrh. Then being divinely warned in a dream that they should not return to Herod, they departed for their own country another way."

Lord, the wise men brought expensive gifts and presented them to Jesus. Inspire us to follow their example and to fall down and worship You and generously to give You gifts that promote work that Honors You.

We pray in Your name!

Amen

A One Minute Daily Scripture and Prayer
for CHRISTMAS

In the 3rd chapter of First
Samuel, verse 10, we read

"Now the Lord came and stood
and called as at other times,
'Samuel! Samuel!' And Samuel
answered, 'Speak, for Your
servant hears.'"

Lord God, make us attentive so
that we can hear the words You
speak as Samuel did. And give
us courage to follow the signs
You give as the Wise Men did.
Let us become Your obedient
servants.

We pray in the Name of Jesus!

Amen

for the New Year

In the 21st chapter of Revelation
verse 5, we read

"Then He who sat on the throne
said, 'Behold, I make all things
new!'"

Lord God, as we are about to
begin a new year, we rely on
Your power to make all things
new: Fill our hearts with new
love; make our relationships new
with hope; create a new justice
in our nation; and renew Your
Spirit in our land and everywhere
on the earth.

We make our prayer in the Name
of Jesus, Who sits upon
the Throne!

Amen

A One Minute Daily Scripture and Prayer
for the New Year

In Psalm 91, verses 11 & 12, we read

"For God will command His angels concerning you to guard you in all your ways. On their hands, they will bear you up, so that you will not dash your foot against a stone."

Mighty God, we praise You for bringing us to this New Year's Eve. We ask You to send Your holy angels to protect all who celebrate and to guide travelers safely home.

We pray in the Name of Jesus.

Amen

for the New Year

In the 13th chapter of Hebrews, verses 2 & 3, we read

"Do not forget to entertain strangers, for by doing so some have unwittingly entertained angels. And remember the prisoners as if chained with them and those who are mistreated."

Generous God, we thank You for all the many blessings You have poured out on us during these Christmas and New Year's holidays. Now help us to imitate Your generosity throughout the new year in our dealings with strangers, prisoners, and with all who are mistreated.

We pray in the name of Jesus, Who was Himself an immigrant!

Amen

A One Minute Daily Scripture and Prayer
for Martin Luther King Day

In the 18th chapter of Deuteronomy, verses 18 & 19, we read

"The Lord said: 'I will raise up for them a prophet...I will put my words in his mouth.... If anyone does not listen to my words that the prophet speaks in my name, I myself will call him to account.'"

Lord God, may Your words, as they come to us through prophetic messengers like Martin Luther King, Jr., fill us with the fire of justice for the oppressed, with the calm of peace for those living in war-ravaged societies, and with the light of compassion for people of all races, languages and creeds.

We pray in the name of Your Son, Jesus, Who gave His life for us!

Amen

for Easter

Thank you for joining me to pray as we celebrate the triumphal entry of Jesus into Jerusalem on Palm Sunday.

In the 12th chapter of John, verses 13 & 14, we read

"So they took branches of palm trees and went out to meet Jesus shouting, 'Hosanna! Blessed is the one who comes in the name of the Lord, the King of Israel.'"

Lord Jesus, my prayer today on this Palm Sunday is that all people of all nations would join the crowd so long ago and shout HOSANNA to YOU our King—save us!

We pray in Your name!

Amen

A One Minute Daily Scripture and Prayer
for Easter

In the 19th chapter of Luke, verses 41 & 42, we read

"And when Jesus drew near and saw the city he wept over it, saying, 'Would that even today you knew the things that make for peace! But now they are hid from your eyes.'"

Thank You, Lord Jesus, for the love your tears expressed for the city of Jerusalem and for its inhabitants. Let us share Your compassion and care for those who dwell in Jerusalem and for all people everywhere.

We pray in your loving name!

Amen

for Easter

In the 14th chapter of Mark,
verses 22 – 24, we read

"And as they were eating, he
took bread, and broke it, and
gave it to them, and said, 'Take;
this is my body.' And he took a
cup, and when he had given
thanks he gave it to them, and
they all drank of it."

On the very night before You
died, Lord Jesus, You
remembered to give thanks to
Your Father over the meal You
shared with Your disciples. Fill
our hearts with gratitude in every
situation for the goodness and
wonder of Your Love.

We pray in Your name, Lord,
with gratitude!

Amen

for Easter

In the 27th chapter of Matthew, verse 29, we read

"…and plaiting a crown of thorns they put it on his head, and put a reed in his right hand. And kneeling before him they mocked him, saying, 'Hail King of the Jews!'"

Forgive us, Lord God, when we, who know Him, fail to stand up for Him when He is being mocked — especially when He is mocked and disrespected in the poor, the unlovely, or refugees. Help each of us to be always ready to proclaim our personal faith and relationship to Jesus to every person and in every situation.

We pray in the name of our Lord and Savior Jesus, Who suffered and died for us!

Amen

for Easter

In the 53rd chapter of Isaiah, verse 3, we read

"He was despised and rejected by others; a man of suffering and acquainted with infirmity; and as one from whom others hide their faces, he was despised, and we held him of no account."

Lord Jesus, You were despised, rejected and held in no account by the powerful people who put You on the Cross. Allow us to acknowledge and show respect to people in our world who are despised and held in no account for whatever reason.

We pray in the name of Jesus, Who died a cruel death so that we can be saved!

Amen

for Easter

In the 14th chapter of Mark,
verse 50, we read

"And they all forsook him and
fled."

Lord Jesus, Your disciples
deserted You and fled when You
were crucified. Give us the
courage we need to stand by
You so that we can begin to
understand a bit more the
ultimate sacrifice You made for
our salvation.

We pray in Your name, Lord of
Love!

Amen

for Easter

In the 40th chapter of Isaiah, verse 5, we read

"Then the glory of the Lord shall be revealed, and all people shall see it together for the mouth of the Lord has spoken."

Lord God, when Your Son, Jesus, rose from the dead on that first Easter morning the prophetic words of Isaiah were fulfilled, for surely in Him Your glory was completely revealed. I thank You that, together with all believers, I have seen this great day of Resurrection.

We pray in the name of Jesus our Risen Lord! Alleluia!

Amen

A One Minute Daily Scripture and Prayer
for Easter

In the 16th chapter of Mark,
verse 9, we read

"Now when he rose early on the
first day of the week, he
appeared first to Mary
Magdalene from whom he had
cast out seven demons."

Lord Jesus, when You rose from
the dead, You revealed Yourself
to Mary Magdalene whom You
delivered from demons. Help us
to see that because You live now
You still open Your arms to
everyone even as You did to
Mary Magdalene.

We pray, Lord, thanking You for
being with us always!

Amen

A One Minute Daily Scripture and Prayer
for Easter

In the 24th chapter of Luke, verse 13, we read

"That very day two of them were going to a village named Emmaus, about seven miles from Jerusalem and talking with each other about all the things that had happened."

As we go about our tasks and journeys, O God, help us to find companions with whom we can talk about all the amazing things You do in our lives. Fill our families and friendships with the Spirit of Your love.

We pray in the name of Jesus, our constant friend!

Amen

for Easter

In the 24th chapter of Luke,
verses 22 & 23, we read

"Moreover, some women of our
company amazed us. They were
at the tomb early in the morning
and did not find his body; and
they came back saying they had
even seen a vision of angels,
who said that he was alive."

Lord Jesus, allow us to be
astounded by the word
of Your Resurrection. When
women or men tell us of the
miraculous things You do in the
power of Your Spirit, open our
minds and hearts to Your
hand at work in our world.

We pray in Your name, Living
Lord!

Amen

for Easter

In the 24th chapter of Luke, verses 45 & 46, we read

"Then Jesus opened their minds to understand the scriptures and said to them, 'Thus it is written that the Christ should suffer and on the third day rise from the dead.'"

Lord Jesus, open our minds and hearts so that we will understand the scriptures today as you did for Your disciples on the day of Your Resurrection, so that as we study we will be led by You. Give us open hearts and minds so that we can hear You speak to us.

We pray in Your name, Jesus our Teacher!

Amen

A One Minute Daily Scripture and Prayer
for Easter

In the 20th chapter of John,
verses 2 & 3, we read

"So Mary Magdalene ran and
went to Simon Peter and the
other disciple, the one whom
Jesus loved, and said to them,
'They have taken the Lord out of
the tomb, and we do not know
where they have laid him.' Peter
then came out with the other
disciple and they went toward
the tomb."

Lord, help us to be so devoted to
You that we will be willing to go
to any lengths, as Mary
Magdalene did, to find You and
to share the good news with
others even when they may
make fun of us.

We pray in Your name, Risen
Savior!

Amen

403

A One Minute Daily Scripture and Prayer
for Easter

In the 20th chapter of John,
verses 8 - 10, we read

"Then the other disciple, who
reached the tomb first, also went
in and he saw and believed; for
as yet they did not know the
scripture, that he must rise from
the dead. Then the disciples
went back to their homes."

Risen Lord, thank You that You
reveal the truth of the scriptures
to us when we listen to You and
open our hearts to accept it.
Open the hearts of all people to
come to
believe the scriptures that tell us
about You and Your teachings.

We pray, Lord Jesus, thanking
You for giving us the scriptures!

Amen

for Easter

In the 1st chapter of Acts, verses
10 & 11, we read

"And while they were gazing into
heaven as Jesus went, behold
two men stood by them in white
robes, and said, 'Men of Galilee
why do you stand looking into
heaven? This Jesus who was
taken up from you into heaven,
will come in the same way as
you saw him go into heaven.'"

Lord Jesus, give us faith to
accept these scriptures and
believe that You revealed
Yourself to men and women
after You rose from the dead and
that they saw You ascend back
into heaven. Let us look at the
sky and hope to see You coming
back as some day You will.

We pray in Your name, Lord
Jesus!

Amen

for the Holy Spirit & Pentecost

In the 14th chapter of John, verse 26, we read

"But the Counselor, the Holy Spirit, whom the Father will send in my name, will teach you all things and bring to your remembrance all that I have said to you"

Father God, send Your Holy Spirit to us now, so that He can guide us to understand all that Jesus teaches us.

We pray in the name of Jesus!

Amen

for the Holy Spirit & Pentecost

In the 16th chapter of John,
verse 13, we read

"When the Spirit of truth comes,
he will guide you into all truth;"

Come, Holy Spirit, to me and
guide me to the truth. Each day
worldly cares try to deceive me,
and so I need Your help.

We pray in the name of Jesus,
Who is the Truth!

Amen

for the Holy Spirit & Pentecost

In the 1st chapter of Acts, verse 8, we read

"You shall be my witnesses in Jerusalem and in Judea and Samaria and to the end of the earth."

Holy Spirit, fill me with Your Power so that I can be a strong witness about Jesus in my town, to my family, to friends and to all to whom You send me.

We pray in the name of Jesus!

Amen

for the Holy Spirit & Pentecost

In the 2nd chapter of Acts,
verses 1, 2, & 4, we read

"When the day of Pentecost had
come, they were all together in
one place. And suddenly a
sound came from heaven like
the rush of a mighty wind, and it
filled the house where they were
sitting—And they were all filled
with the Holy Spirit and began to
speak in other tongues, as the
Spirit gave them utterance."

Lord, lead us today to come
together, as your disciples did
long ago, and open our hearts so
that we can receive more fully
the gift of Your Holy Spirit.

We pray in the name of Jesus!

Amen

A One Minute Daily Scripture and Prayer
for the Holy Spirit & Pentecost

In the 2nd chapter of Acts, verse 17, we read

"And in the last days it shall be, God declares, that I will pour out my Spirit upon all flesh."

Lord God, I reach out to You now, and I ask You to pour out Your Holy Spirit on me, on all my family and friends, and on Your church wherever it meets so that we can be bold witnesses for You.

We pray in the name of Jesus!

Amen

for the Holy Spirit & Pentecost

In the 14th chapter of John,
verse 26, we read

"But the Comforter who is the
Holy Spirit whom the Father will
send in my name, he will teach
you all things, and bring all
things to your remembrance,
whatever I have said to you."

Lord, broaden our understanding
of all the ways the Holy Spirit
works in our lives. Help us to
see Him as our Comforter,
teacher, leader of our thoughts,
and revealer of what you say to
us.

We pray in the name of Jesus!

Amen

for the Holy Spirit & Pentecost

In the 11th chapter of Luke,
verse 13, we read

"If you then, who are evil, know
how to give good gifts to your
children, how much more will the
heavenly Father give the Holy
Spirit to those who ask him!"

Father in heaven, lead us, as we
pray, to ask for the gift of the
Holy Spirit, Who will guide us in
Your will and Who will empower
us to live as You would have us
to live.

We pray in the name of Jesus!

Amen

412

for the Holy Spirit & Pentecost

In the 2nd chapter of First Corinthians, verses 4 – 13, we read

"But God has revealed them unto us by his Spirit; for the Spirit searches all things of God. Which things also we speak not in the words which man's wisdom teaches, but which the Holy Spirit teaches; comparing spiritual things with spiritual."

Lord, when we seek to understand things we can't fully comprehend, let us ask the Holy Spirit to teach us for He can reveal things to us spiritually and He will lead us each day to fuller experience of Your truth and goodness.

We pray in the name of Jesus!

Amen

for the Holy Spirit & Pentecost

In the 1st chapter of Acts, verses 8 & 12, we read

"Jesus said to His disciples, 'You will receive power when the Holy Spirit comes upon you, and you will be my witnesses…to the ends of the earth.'…Then they returned to Jerusalem."

Lord Jesus, after Your Ascension, Your disciples waited expectantly in Jerusalem for the gift of the Holy Spirit. As we await Pentecost, when Churches celebrate the descent of Your Spirit, make our hearts & minds ready to receive His power so that we and our world will be healed and transformed.

We pray in Your holy Name!

Amen

414

for the Holy Spirit & Pentecost

In the 2nd chapter of Acts, verse 4, we read

"And they were all filled with the Holy Spirit and began to speak in other tongues as the Spirit gave them utterance."

Lord Jesus, fill us with Your Holy Spirit so that we will receive the gifts that He chooses to give to us.

We pray in the Your Holy name!

Amen

for the Holy Spirit & Pentecost

In the 2nd chapter of Acts,
verses 1 - 4, we read

"When the time for Pentecost
was fulfilled…suddenly there
came from the sky…a strong
driving wind, and…there
appeared to them tongues as of
fire…. And they were all filled
with the Holy Spirit!"

Lord Holy Spirit, fill each of us
with Your Divine Presence. Give
us perseverance to walk every
day in the path Jesus has set out
for us. Give us courage to meet
every challenge that comes our
way. Give us openness to
receive Your healing in our
bodies, minds, memories, and
spirits. And give us confidence to
work mighty deeds for Your
glory.

We pray, Father, in the Name of
Jesus, through the Holy Spirit!

Amen

A One Minute Daily Scripture and Prayer
for the Holy Spirit & Pentecost

In the 8th chapter of Romans, verses 26 & 27, we read

"The Spirit comes to the aid of our weakness; for we do not know how to pray as we ought, but the Spirit Himself… intercedes for the holy ones according to God's will."

In our weakness we cry out to You, Lord Holy Spirit, begging for Your intercession on our behalf. We join our prayers with Your Divine prayer for our families, for the sick, for those who are homeless & for those who are strangers in a foreign land; touch us all according to God's will!

We pray in the Name of Jesus!

Amen

A One Minute Daily Scripture and Prayer
for Graduation

In the 3rd chapter of Proverbs, verses 13 & 14, we read

"Happy is the man who finds wisdom and the man who gets understanding. For the gain from it is better than the gain from silver and its profit better than gold."

God of wisdom, in this season where young people are graduating from schools and going out into the world, help them to make wise decisions and to grow into persons of understanding.

We pray in the name of Jesus!

Amen

A One Minute Daily Scripture and Prayer
for those who died for their country

In the 15th chapter of John, verse 13, we read

"Greater love has no man than this, that he lay down his life for his friends."

Lord, as we honor those throughout our history who have given their lives for our country, help us to honor them and give our lives to promote peace and justice in the whole world.

We pray in the name of Jesus!

Amen

for those who died for their country

In the 6th chapter of Numbers, verses 24 & 26, we read

"The Lord bless you and keep you!…The Lord look kindly upon you and give you peace!"

Lord God, we ask that You send Your peace to all those who have given their lives serving the causes of justice for their nation.

We ask, too, that You keep travelers safe and fill all families with Your blessings.

We pray in the Name of Jesus!

Amen

for Mothers

In the 1st chapter of First Samuel, verses 27 & 28, we read the words of Hannah, the mother of the Prophet Samuel

"For this child I prayed; and the Lord has granted me my petition which I made to Him. Therefore I have given him to the Lord; as long as he lives, he is given to the Lord."

Lord, I pray for all those who want children but have none. Help them to ask You to send children to them. May all mothers follow Hannah's example and dedicate their children to You.

We pray in Your name!

Amen

A One Minute Daily Scripture and Prayer
for Mothers

In the 30th chapter of Proverbs, verses 20, 25, 28 – 30, we read

"She opens her arms to the poor and extends her hands to the needy… She is clothed with strength and dignity; she can laugh at the days to come…. Her children arise and call her blessed; her husband also, and he praises her; many women do noble things but you surpass them all….Charm is deceptive and beauty is fleeting, but a woman who fears the Lord is to be praised."

Dear Lord, may these words of Scripture be the desire of every Mother's heart. Give Mothers all they need to be just, loving and strong.

We ask it, Father, in the name of Jesus!

Amen

A One Minute Daily Scripture and Prayer
for Fathers

In the 5th chapter of
Deuteronomy, verse 16, we read

"Honor your Father and your
mother as the Lord your God
commanded you."

Father, God, we ask You to
bless all Fathers – biological,
adoptive, and spiritual. Meet
the needs of all Fathers.

We pray in the name of Jesus!

Amen

for Fathers

In the 1st chapter of Luke,
verses 14 - 17 we read

"And you (Zechariah) will have
joy and gladness, and many will
rejoice at John's birth for he will
be great before the Lord, and he
shall drink no wine nor strong
drink, and he will be filled with
the Holy Spirit even from his
mother's womb, and he will turn
many of the sons of Israel to the
Lord their God—to make ready
for the Lord a people prepared."

Oh Lord, help all Fathers to
rejoice when they have children
and to teach their children by
word and example to give their
lives to serve You, as Zechariah
did for his son John.

We pray in Your name, Father!

Amen

for Grandparents & extended family

In 2nd Timothy, chapter 1, verses 3 & 5, we read

"I thank God…when I call to remembrance the genuine faith that is in you, which dwelt first in your grandmother Lois and your mother Eunice, and I am persuaded is in you also."

God of our ancestors, we thank You for the examples of faith and love that so many have received from the lives of grandparents, parents, aunts, uncles and other family members. Reward them each for the goodness they have shown us.

We pray in the Name of Jesus, Who lived as a Child in the home of Mary and Joseph!

Amen

A One Minute Daily Scripture and Prayer
for Laborers

In the 11th chapter of Matthew verse, 28 we read

"Come to Me all you who labor and are heavy laden, and I will give you rest."

On this Labor Day, Lord, we honor all who earn their living by the sweat of their brow, and we ask You to help them to come to Jesus Who welcomes them and promises to give them rest. May we be careful to give them a just wage as well as offer them time for rest as Jesus does.

We pray in Your name, Just Lord!

Amen

for Thanksgiving Day

In Psalm 136, verses 1 – 3, we read

"O give thanks to the Lord, for he is good, for his steadfast love endures forever. O give thanks to the God of Gods, for his steadfast love endures forever, O give thanks to the Lord of lords, for his steadfast love endures forever"

Mighty Lord of Lords, we come to You on this Thanksgiving Day, and we stand amazed that You are so good to us and that You love us with a steadfast-Love. We thank You, and we ask You to let our love be like Yours for our family, friends and for everyone.

We pray in the name of Jesus, Who is Love!

Amen

for when we are Anxious

In the 10th chapter of Luke,
verses 39, 40B - 42, we read

"And Martha had a sister called
Mary, who sat at the Lord's feet
and listened to his teaching….
Martha said, 'Tell Mary to help
me.' But the Lord answered her,
'Martha, Martha, you are anxious
and troubled about many things;
Mary has chosen the good
portion, which shall not be taken
from her.'"

Dear Lord, when I get anxious
about duties I have like, cleaning
the house, help me to do as
Mary did and go aside to spend
time listening to You.

We pray in Your name!

Amen

for when we are Anxious

In Psalm 30, verses 2 & 3, we read

"O Lord my God, I called to you for help and you healed me. O Lord, you brought me up from the grave, you spared me from going down into the pit."

Thank You, Lord, that all of us — whatever our race or gender or economic situation — all of us can call out to You for help and You always hear us: You heal us when we are sick, You lift us up when we are in terrible trouble. We cry out to You now for all those who are suffering and we lift them up to You; fill them and us with Your peace and calming Spirit.

We ask it, Father, in the name of Jesus.

Amen

for when we are Anxious

In the 5th chapter of Acts, verse 19, we read

"But at night an angel of the Lord opened the prison doors and brought them out."

Lord, when we are faced with trials that seem impossible give us the assurance of Your love and power to meet our needs. Send angels to rescue us and to renew our trust in Your care for us.

We pray in the name of Jesus!

Amen

for when we are Anxious

In the 6th chapter of Galatians, verses 8 – 10, we read

"For he who sows to his own flesh will from the flesh reap corruption; but he who sows to the Spirit will from the Spirit reap eternal life. And let us not grow weary in well-doing, for in due season we will reap, if we do not lose heart. So then, as we have opportunity, let us do good to all men, and especially to those who are of the household of faith."

O Lord, when I grow weary in my efforts to do the right things, help me to put all my hope and trust in the guidance of the Holy Spirit so that my worrying will cease and Your peace will fill my life now and eternally.

We pray in the name of the Father, Jesus and the Holy Spirit!

Amen

for when we are Anxious

In the 8th chapter of Romans, verses 23 & 24, we read

"Not only the creation, but we ourselves, who have the first fruits of the Spirit, grown inwardly as we wait for adoption as sons, the redemption of our bodies. For in this hope we were saved."

O Lord, there are times in all our lives when we must face trials, and we long to escape them, but with the help of the Holy Spirit Who gives us the first fruits of love and faith, we realize that our hope is in You and that our bodies will be redeemed and we will live eternally with You in the glory of heaven.

We pray in the name of Jesus, our Savior!

Amen

A One Minute Daily Scripture and Prayer
for when we are Anxious

In the 41st chapter of Isaiah, verse 10, we read

"'Fear not, for I am with you; be not dismayed, for I am Your God. I will strengthen you; yes, I will help you, I will uphold you with My righteous right hand.'"

Dear Lord, thank You for these words of assurance; help all people who are suffering from natural disasters, war and oppression to reach out and claim Your promise. And help all of us to put our trust in You, especially in times when we don't understand why bad or difficult things happen.

We pray in Your name, Lord of comfort and provision!

Amen

for when we are Anxious

In the 6th chapter of Numbers, verses 24 - 26, we read

"The Lord bless you and keep you; the Lord make his face shine upon you and be gracious to you; the Lord turn his face toward you and give you peace."

Precious and loving Lord, thank You for the blessings that these words from scripture give. May the peace and calm and the trust that You offer us in these words rest on each of us and on all those we love.

We pray in Your name, Lord of endless blessings!

Amen

for when we are Anxious

In the 17th chapter of Jeremiah, verse 7, we read

"But blessed is the man who trusts in the Lord, whose confidence is in him."

Precious Lord, when we feel that everything is going wrong in our country and in our lives, help us to look to You and to remember all the things You do every day that allow us to make it through our trials.   Renew our faith so that we can put all our hope and confidence in You, for You alone can save us.

We pray in Your name, saving God!

Amen

for when we are Anxious

In the 1st chapter of Joshua, verse 9, we read

"Have I not commanded You? Be strong and courageous. Do not be terrified; do not be discouraged, for the Lord Your God will be with you wherever you go."

Dear Lord, give us courage and strength so that when we face trials or dangers, we will be filled with calm assurance that You are with us wherever we go and that Your protection in every moment will keep us safe.

We pray in gratitude to You, our strong God!

Amen

for when we are Anxious

In the 1st chapter of Isaiah,
verse 18, we read

"Come now, let us reason
together, says the Lord. Though
your sins are like scarlet, they
shall be as white as snow;
though they are red as crimson
they shall be like wool."

Thank You, Lord, for this
wonderful promise: that You
will forgive us for even the
greatest sins we have
committed. Give us confidence
that Your mercy extends
even to us who are sinners.

We pray in humble gratitude,
forgiving God!

Amen

for when we are Anxious

In the 20th chapter of John, verses 19 & 20, we read

"On the evening of that day, the first day of the week, the doors being shut where the disciples were for fear of the Jews, Jesus came and stood among them and said to them, 'Peace be with you.' When he had said this, he showed them his hands and his side. Then the disciples were glad when they saw the Lord."

Help us today, Lord, when we are in need of peace or healing to open the doors of our hearts and invite You to come in so we can receive the peace and healing You give.

We pray in the name of Jesus, our Healer!

Amen

for the Lord's Guidance

In the 16th chapter of Acts, verse 22, we read

"The crowd joined in the attacks against Paul and Silas, and the magistrates ordered them to be stripped and beaten."

O Lord, help us to listen to You so that when the crowds where we are call for things to be done that we know are not right we will have courage to stand against the wrong doing.

We pray in Your name, Lord Jesus!

Amen

for the Lord's Guidance

In the 11th chapter of Hebrews, verse 8, we read

"Abraham trusted God, and when God told him to leave home and go far away to another land which He promised to give to him, Abraham obeyed. Away he went not even knowing where he was going."

Dear Lord, forgive us when we fail to trust You about what we should do — even about small things, like whether we should apologize to a person about whom we have talked badly. Give us faith to obey You in everything each day, as Abraham did. Give us confidence that You will show us the way as You did for Abraham.

We pray in Your name, all-knowing God!

Amen

440

A One Minute Daily Scripture and Prayer
for the Lord's Guidance

In Psalm 97, verse 2, we read

"Clouds and thick darkness surround him; righteousness is the foundation of his throne."

O Lord, You are so deep and righteous that we fail to know Who you truly are. Fill us with Your Holy Spirit so that He can open our understanding of Who You are and what You want us to do each day, through the words of the Bible which we read.

We pray in Your name, Holy Lord!

Amen

for the Lord's Guidance

In the 13th chapter of John,
verse 37, we read

"Peter said to Jesus, 'Lord, why
can't I follow you now? I will lay
down my life for you.'"

O Lord, teach us to be willing to
wait until we have prayed and
listened to You before we make
any decision, especially the big
ones in life, like 'should we stay
in a place or move.' Deepen
our confidence in the sure
knowledge that You have a time
and place for everything and in
You, all will be right.

We pray in Your name, all-
knowing God!

Amen

for the Lord's Guidance

In the 5th chapter of First Thessalonians, verse 23, we read

"And may the God of peace Himself sanctify you through and through— that is separate you from profane things, make you pure and wholly consecrated to God— and may your spirit and soul and body be preserved sound and complete (and found) blameless at the coming of our Lord Jesus Christ, the Messiah."

Lord, lead us to realize the depths of what it means when You forgive our sins and call us to separate ourselves from worldly ways and be wholly consecrated to You. Fill us with Your Holy Spirit Who will help us to know best how to follow You.

We pray in the name of the Father, Jesus, and the Holy Spirit!

Amen

443

for the Lord's Guidance

In the 17th chapter of Proverbs, verse 27, we read

"A man of knowledge uses words with restraint, and a man of understanding is even-tempered."

Dear Lord, help us to be slow to lash out or to speak words that are unwise or unkind, especially when we are tempted by circumstances to do so. Give us an even-temper, so that we will be able to use words of understanding and compassion before we speak.

We pray in Your name, wise God!

Amen

for the Lord's Guidance

In the 4th chapter of Ephesians, verse 2, we read

"…with all lowliness and meekness, with patience, forbearing with one another in love."

Dear Lord, help us to live these words of Scripture in concrete ways, rather than just reading them. Make us want to be humble and meek in our judgments and words; make us want to be patient with other people — even with those we do not care for — make us want to bear with others in the spirit of love, especially with our families, friends, and co-workers.

We pray in Your name, Lord Jesus, Who are our perfect example.

Amen

for the Lord's Guidance

In the 1st chapter of Jonah,
verses 2 – 3A, we read

"Go to the great city of Nineveh
and preach against it, because
its wickedness has come up
before me. But Jonah ran away
from the Lord and headed for
Tarshish."

O Lord, forgive us for those
times when, even though we
hear Your call, we go in the
opposite direction. Remind us
that Your call is always a call of
love and that our truest
happiness comes when we say
yes to You.

We pray in Your name Lord,
Who graciously forgives us!

Amen

A One Minute Daily Scripture and Prayer
for the Lord's Guidance

In the 9th chapter of Daniel,
verse 9A, we read

"The Lord our God is merciful
and forgiving."

Dear Lord, help us to model our
relations with other people after
Your perfect example of
compassion and forgiveness.

We pray in Your name, perfect
God!

Amen

for the Lord's Guidance

In the 18th chapter of John, verse 37, we read

"Pilate said to Jesus, 'So you are a king?' Jesus answered, 'You say that I am a king. For this I was born, and for this I have come into the world, to bear witness to the truth. Everyone who is of the truth hears my voice.'"

Lord, help us to discern between truth and lies. And then let us avoid lies and liars at all costs so that we will listen to the Truth which is Your voice speaking to us clearly.

We pray in Your name, Lord Who are Truth!

Amen

for the Lord's Guidance

In the 3rd chapter of Philippians, verse 12, we read

"I don't mean to say I am perfect. I haven't learned all I should even yet, but I keep working toward that day when I will finally be all that Christ saved me for and wants me to be."

Dear Lord, oh, how I want to be more like You; yet I am still far from the goal. Give me all the graces I need to work daily to achieve my desire to be all You created me to be.

We pray in Your name, Jesus, our perfect Lord!

Amen

for the Lord's Guidance

In the 28th chapter of Matthew, verses 16 – 18, we read

"Now the eleven disciples went to Galilee, to the mountain Jesus had directed them. And when they saw him they worshipped him; but some doubted. And Jesus came and said to them, 'All authority in heaven and on earth has been given to me.'"

Lord, Your disciples did what You told them to do and You appeared to them as You promised. Please help us to be willing to do whatever You tell us to do, even when it does not seem to be possible, and help us to trust that You know what is best.

We pray, Jesus, in Your all-knowing name!

Amen

for the Lord's Guidance

In the 2nd chapter of Titus,
verses 2 & 3, we read

"Tell the older men to be
temperate, serious, prudent,
and sound in faith, in love, and in
endurance. Likewise, tell the
older women to be reverent in
behavior."

Lord God, as we grow older, let
us focus our energies on
receiving the gifts about which
Titus writes. Rather than looking
to the past, fill our lives with the
hope of becoming ever more
reverent, faithful and loving.

We pray in the Name of Jesus!

Amen

for Healing

In the 3rd chapter of Acts, verses 6 & 7, we read

"But Peter said, 'I have no silver and gold, but I give you what I have; in the name of Jesus Christ of Nazareth, walk.' And he took the cripple man by the right hand and raised him up; and immediately his feet and ankles were made strong."

Lord God, send us today, people like Peter, who are willing to be channels of Your healing power.

We pray in the name of Jesus, our Healer!

Amen

for Healing

In the 9th chapter of Matthew, verses 20 – 22, we read

"And behold, a woman who had suffered from a hemorrhage for twelve years came up behind him and touched the fringe of his garment; for she said to herself, 'If I only touch his garment, I shall be made well.' Jesus turned, and seeing her he said, 'Take heart daughter; your faith has made you well.' And instantly the woman was made well."

Lord Jesus, You are our Healer. Give us the faith we need to reach out to You when we are sick and to believe, as the woman in scripture did, that You will heal us when we ask in faith, for You are the same yesterday today and forever.

We pray in faith, Lord Jesus!

Amen

for Healing

In Psalm 30, verses 1 & 2 and verses 11 & 12, we read

"I will extol you, O Lord, for you have drawn me up, and did not let my foes rejoice over me. O Lord my God, I cried to you for help, and you have healed me. You have turned my mourning into dancing—and clothed me with joy, so that my soul may praise you and not be silent. O Lord my God, I will give thanks to you forever."

Lord, I pray for all those who need your healing touch: fill them with Your healing power. Let them rejoice in their healing, thanking You for delivering them, and let them give You praise and glory all the days of their lives.

We ask it, O God, in the name of Jesus, our Healer!

Amen

A One Minute Daily Scripture and Prayer
for Healing

In the 4th chapter of Matthew, verse 24, we read

"So Jesus' fame spread throughout all Syria and they brought to him all the sick, those who were afflicted with various diseases and pains, demoniacs, epileptics, and paralytics, and he cured them."

Lord Jesus, give us faith today to come to You when we are sick and to ask You to heal us as You did when You were on the earth. Because You are the same today as You were then and as You always will be, help us to be confident in Your desire to heal us now and to believe in Your power.

We pray in Your Healing name!

Amen

for Healing

In Psalm 41, verses 1 – 3, we read

"Happy are those who consider the poor; the Lord delivers them in the day of trouble. The Lord protects them and keeps them alive; they are called happy in the land. You do not give them up to the will of their enemies. The Lord sustains them on their sick-bed; in their illness you heal all their infirmities."

Precious Lord, give us the wisdom to follow Your word and to be helpful to the poor with our prayers, presence and wealth. Then we can claim that word which tells us that we will be happy, and that You will protect us and heal us when we are sick.

We pray in Your name, Healing Lord!

Amen

456

for Praising God

In the 20th chapter of Jeremiah, verse 13, we read

"Sing to the Lord! Praise the Lord! For though I was poor and needy, he rescued me from my oppressors."

Lord Jesus, my heart is full of praises for You because I know You are kind and compassionate, and because I know Your love and protection extends to every person black, brown, white, poor, rich, indeed to every person.

We pray in Your name, Lord of all!

Amen

for Praising God

In the 1st chapter of Luke,
verses 46 – 48, we read

"And Mary said, 'My soul glorifies
the Lord and my spirit rejoices in
God my Savior, for he has been
mindful of the humble state of
his servant.'"

Lord Jesus, let each of us praise
You with humble hearts, like
Mary's, for all the many
blessings You give us each day
– air to breath, eyes to see, and
above all, Your wonderful gift of
having You as our Savior!

We pray in Your name, Lord of
all!

Amen

for Praising God

In the 3rd chapter of Acts, verse 25, we read

"You are the sons of the prophets and of the covenant which God gave to your fathers, saying to Abraham, 'And in your posterity shall all the families of the earth be blessed.'"

I praise You, Father, that You sent Jesus Your Son to bless all the families of the earth. Let His message of faith, love, justice, and peace be received world-wide.

We pray in His name!

Amen

for Praising God

In the 4th chapter of Mark, verse 10, we read

"Afterwards, when Jesus was alone with the Twelve and with His other disciples, they asked Him, 'What does your story mean.'"

Dear Lord, I praise and thank You because You have taught me so many things that I did not understand, especially when I have experienced trials in my life. I rejoice that You enlarge the depth of my understanding when I go alone, away from interruptions, with only You, and in those moments of quiet and solitude, I can ask You to tell me all You want me to know from the trial or pain that I was going through. My heart and my whole being are filled with wonder and awe, praise and thanksgiving for the gift of Your Presence in my life in those times!

We pray in Your name, Lord Jesus!

Amen

for Praising God

In the 15th chapter of First
Corinthians, verse 10A,
we read

"But by the grace of God I am
what I am."

O dear Lord, how I rejoice in the
sure knowledge that You have
created me because of Your
boundless mercy and favor;
thank You for allowing us to be
called Your children. Help us to
celebrate this gift and to work
every day to bear fruit for Your
glory.

We pray in Your name, Lord
Jesus!

Amen

461

for courage to Help Others

In the 10th chapter of Luke, verses 25 and following, we read

"An expert in the law asked Jesus, 'What must I do to inherit eternal life?' Jesus answered, 'What is written in the law?' He replied, 'Love the Lord your God with all your heart and with all your soul and with all your strength and with all your mind and, love your neighbor as yourself.' Jesus replied, 'Do this and you will live.' The expert in the law said, 'And who is my neighbor?' (Jesus tells the story of the Good Samaritan.) Jesus then asks, 'Which of the three do you think proved neighbor to the victim?' The law expert replied, 'The one who showed mercy.' And Jesus said, 'Go and do likewise.'"

Lord, help me to know that when I am helping victims of violence or oppression, I am loving you with all my heart, mind, soul and strength.

We pray in the name of Jesus!

Amen

462

for courage to Help Others

In Psalm 143, verse 1, we read

"O Lord hear my prayer; in your faithfulness and righteousness come to my relief."

Mighty Lord, we lift up our hearts and prayers to You as the psalmist did long ago. We ask You to make our concern real so that we will assist in concrete ways all those who are in trouble because of hurricanes, earthquakes, fires and other natural disasters; give them relief, comfort and profound assurance of Your love, care and provision for them each day.

We pray in Your name, caring Lord Jesus!

Amen

for courage to Help Others

In the 15th chapter of John, verse 17, we read

"This is my command; Love each other."

Dear Lord, thank You that we see so many people coming to aid the people of Texas who have been devastated in the floods of hurricane Harvey. Bless each one who has given their time and energy to help those in need. Touch our hearts to do the things we can to help and truly love our neighbors as You command us to do.

We pray in the name of Jesus, Who is Love!

Amen

for courage to Help Others

In the 25th chapter of Matthew,
verses 44 & 45, we read

"Then they will reply, 'Lord, when
did we ever see You hungry or
thirsty or a stranger or naked or
sick or in prison and not help
You?' And I will answer, 'When
you refused to help the least of
these My brothers, you were
refusing help to Me.'"

O Lord, give us hearts of love
and compassion for all those
who are hurting so that we will
reach out to help them. Make us
realize that when we help others,
we are helping You.

We pray in Your name, Lord of
Love!

Amen

for courage to Help Others

In the 31st chapter of Proverbs, verses 8 & 9, we read

"Speak out for those who cannot speak, for the rights of all the destitute. Speak out, judge righteously, defend the rights of the poor and needy."

O Lord, give all of us who live in a country where we can speak out for those less fortunate, the courage to be known as people who defend the rights of the poor and needy.

We pray in the name of Jesus, Who gave His life for every person, poor and rich alike!

Amen

for courage to Help Others

In the 2nd chapter of Acts,
verses 44 & 45, we read

"And all who believed were
together and had all things in
common; and they sold their
possessions and goods and
distributed to all, as any had
need."

Lord God, help us to become
more like the first followers of
Your Son, Jesus, whose Spirit-
filled generosity enabled them to
help meet the material needs of
Your people.

We pray in the name of Jesus,
Who gave His all on the cross for
us!

Amen

for courage to Help Others

In the 4th chapter of Philippians, verses 6 & 7, we read

"Be anxious for nothing, but in everything by prayer and supplication, with thanksgiving let your requests be made known to God; and the peace of God which surpasses all understanding, will guard your hearts and minds through Christ Jesus."

Lord, my heart goes out to all those who are suffering terrible loss because of floods, fires, earthquakes, famine, war or violence, so I offer my prayer for them. Cover them with Your peace, assuring them that You are with them, walking through their trials and reminding them that You will never leave them.

We pray in Your name, Loving God!

Amen

A One Minute Daily Scripture and Prayer
for courage to Help Others

In the 1st chapter of
Deuteronomy, verse 17, we read

"Do not show partiality in
judging; hear both small and
great alike."

Dear Lord, help us to treat all
people fairly in our actions
towards them, in our thoughts
and in our words about them.
Keep us from seeing the faults of
those we do not like as greater
than the faults of people we do
like. Let us be impartial to each
person great or small.

We pray in Your name, just God!

Amen

for courage to Help Others

In the 19th chapter of Leviticus,
verse 13, we read

"Do not defraud your neighbor or
rob him."

Dear Lord, help all of us, and
especially people in high places,
to hear these words that You
have spoken to us in scripture.
Change our hearts and minds so
that we will not cheat or oppress
any person, and so that we will
pay those who work for us justly.

We pray in Your name, righteous
God!

Amen

for courage to Help Others

In the 3rd chapter of First Kings, verse 9, we read

"So give your servant a discerning heart to govern your people and to distinguish between right and wrong. For who is able to govern this great people of yours?"

O Lord, move in a mighty way on the men and women who are responsible for governing our great country and help them to humble themselves; give them humility so that they can receive from You the gift of a discerning heart and to know right from wrong, as they govern.

We pray in the name of Jesus!

Amen

for courage to Help Others

In the 3rd chapter of First
Corinthians, verse 9, we read

"For we are fellow workmen—
joint promoters, laborers,
together —with and for God;
you are God's garden and
vineyard and field under
cultivation; you are God's
building."

Thank You, Lord, for the
privilege of being a fellow
worker with You in cultivating the
community of Your people.
Help us to do our best to be
obedient to You in this work.

We pray in Your name, Master
Builder!

Amen

for courage to Help Others

In the 13th chapter of Hebrews,
verses 1 & 2, we read

"Let brotherly love continue. Do
not neglect to show hospitality to
strangers, for thereby some have
entertained angels unaware."

Lord, give us the graces we
need, both as individuals
and as a nation, to open our
hearts and our doors to
everyone, for otherwise, we
might miss an opportunity
to entertain Your angels.

We pray in Your name Lord,
Who open Your arms to all!

Amen

for courage to Help Others

In the 13th chapter of Hebrews,
verse 3, we read

"Don't forget about those in jail.
Suffer with them as though you
were there yourself. Share the
sorrow of those being
mistreated, for you know what
they are going through."

Lord, touch our hearts to have
compassion for those in prison,
most especially to be mindful of
those who are unjustly deprived
of their freedom; help us to pray
for them and bless all who are
involved in prison ministries.

We pray in Your name, Lord of
compassion!

Amen

for courage to Help Others

In the 4th chapter of Joel, verse
16, we read

"The heavens and the earth
quake, but the Lord is a refuge to
his people, a stronghold to the
people of Israel."

O God, move our hearts to
support with our prayers, our
efforts, and our financial
resources, all whose lives have
been decimated by earthquakes,
hurricanes, floods and fires —in
Texas, Florida, Mexico, India,
Canada and everywhere in the
world.

We pray in Your name, O God
our Refuge!

Amen

for courage to Help Others

In Psalm 34, verse 18, we read

"The Lord is near to the broken-hearted, and saves the crushed spirit."

Lord, we lift up all those who are broken in their bodies, spirits, and emotions because of public shootings, violence against family members, murder, or rape. We ask You to bring healing, consolation, human support, and justice to victims and perpetrators, for You, oh Lord, are our Healer and our Hope.

We pray in Your name, Lord Jesus!

Amen

for courage to Help Others

In the 21st chapter of Luke,
verses 2 – 4, we read

"Jesus saw a poor widow put in
two copper coins. And he said,
'Truly I tell you this poor widow
has put in more than all of them;
for they all contributed out of
their abundance, but she out of
her poverty put in all that she
had.'"

Thank You Lord, for the example
of the widow who gave all she
had to live on; make us
generous with our time and
financial resources.

We pray in Your name, generous
Lord!

Amen

for courage to Help Others

In the 3rd chapter of Second
Chronicles, verse 1, we read

"Then Solomon began to build
the temple of the Lord in
Jerusalem on Mount Moriah,
where the Lord had appeared to
his father David. It was on
the threshing floor of Araunah,
the Jebusite, the place provided
by David."

Help us always, Lord, to be
building up Your house in our
lives, by being present at
services, by praying for the
Churches and those who serve
in all sorts of ministries, and by
contributing our money to the
ministries of the Churches.

We pray in Your name, Lord of
the Church!

Amen

for the discipline to pray

In the 6th chapter of Ephesians, verse 18, we read

"Pray at all times in the Spirit, with all prayer and supplication. To that end keep alert with all perseverance, making supplication for all the saints."

Dear Lord, I bow before You and I humbly ask You to help me persevere in prayer for all those who are on the battlefield, working to spread the good news that Jesus is Lord. I lift them to You and beg You to protect them from evil and to prosper their work to give You glory!

I ask it in the name of the Father, Jesus, and the Holy Spirit.

Amen

for the discipline to pray

In the 1st chapter of Acts, verses 13 & 14, we read

"…they went to the upper room where they were staying, Peter & John & James & Andrew & Philip & Thomas…. All these devoted themselves with one accord to prayer, together with some women, and Mary the mother of Jesus, and his brothers."

Lord Jesus, as Your mother Mary and Your disciples waited in the upper room for the coming of the Holy Spirit which You promised, they devoted themselves to prayer. We ask You to strengthen our prayer life and to fill us with Your Holy Spirit so that our prayers will have His power.

We pray in Your holy Name!

Amen

for the discipline to pray

In the 3rd chapter of Acts, verse 19, we read

"Repent therefore, and turn again, that your sins may be blotted out, that times of refreshing may come from the presence of the Lord."

Holy Spirit, lead each of us to know the joy of spending time each day in fellowship with You in prayer because as we pray we live in Your presence.

We pray in the name of Jesus!

Amen

481

for the discipline to pray

In the 6th chapter of Matthew, verse 6, we read

"But when you pray, go away by yourself, all alone and shut the door behind you and pray to your Father secretly, and your Father, who knows your secrets, will reward you."

Precious Lord Jesus Christ, give me the desire and courage each day to go aside from all life's pulls on me and spend time alone in Your Presence, quietly listening and talking to You.

We pray in Your name!

Amen

for the discipline to pray

In the 14th chapter of John,
verses 18 & 19, we read

"Whatever you ask in my name, I
will do it, that the Father may be
glorified in the Son, if you ask
anything in my name, I will do it."

Lord, when I pray help me to ask
for others to know You, for
health and wisdom to serve You
better, and that my family and all
my friends will live in Your will
and Your ways.

We pray in Your name!

Amen

A One Minute Daily Scripture and Prayer
for the discipline to pray

In the 11th chapter of Luke, verses 1 & 2, we read

"Lord teach us to pray. And Jesus said, 'Father, hallowed be thy name. Thy kingdom come. Give us each day our daily bread; and forgive us our sins, for we ourselves forgive everyone who is indebted to us, and lead us not into temptation."

Oh Lord, help me each day to pray this prayer from my heart, and give me every grace I need to fashion my life in ways that will bring Your kingdom here, where I live.

We pray in Your holy name!

Amen

for the discipline to pray

In the 14th chapter of Acts, verse 31, we read

"And when they had prayed, the place in which they were gathered together was shaken; and they were all filled with the Holy Spirit and spoke the word of God with boldness."

Thank You, Lord, for giving us the gift of prayer which keeps us close to You. Fill us with Your Holy Spirit Who guides our prayer.

We pray in the name of Jesus!

Amen

for the discipline to pray

In the 18th chapter of Matthew,
verse 20, we read

"For where two or three are
gathered in my name, there am I
in the midst of them."

Thank You, Precious Lord, for
the privilege of joining with
others to pray, and knowing the
great joy that You are present
with us, hearing us, and giving
us Your gifts of love that sustain
us in all we do.

We pray in Your name, Lord
Jesus!

Amen

A One Minute Daily Scripture and Prayer
for the discipline to pray

In the 4th chapter of Mark, verse 34, we read

"In fact, He taught only by illustrations in His public teaching, but afterwards, when He was alone with His disciples, He would explain His meaning to them."

Dear Lord, there are many of Your teachings that I don't fully understand. Take me alone, with only You, and open my ears and understanding to hear You clearly and personally so that I can come to know better the meanings of Your teaching; teach me in prayer as You did for Your disciples.

We pray in Your name, great Teacher!

Amen

for the discipline to pray

In the 33rd chapter of Second Chronicles, verses 12 – 13A, we read

"In his distress he sought the favor of the Lord his God and humbled himself greatly before the God of his fathers. And when he prayed to him, the Lord was moved by his entreaty and listened to his plea;"

Precious Lord, thank You for being willing to hear us when we pray. Teach us to humble ourselves and to pray earnestly, begging You for our needs, believing You hear our cries, and knowing that You give us the things which are best for us, because You are a compassionate God.

We pray in Your name, Lord of Love!

Amen

A One Minute Daily Scripture and Prayer
for Surrendering to God

In the 1st chapter of Philippians,
verse 20, we read

"For I live in eager expectation
and hope that I will never do
anything that will cause me to be
ashamed of myself; but that I will
always be ready to speak out
boldly for Christ while I am going
through all these trials here, just
as I have in the past; and that I
will always be an honor to Christ,
whether I live or die."

Lord, give us courage and
determination each day to
surrender our will to You so that
You will be in charge of
everything we do, think and say,
so that we will give
all honor to You alone.

We pray in the name of Jesus,
Who surrendered His all for our
salvation!

Amen

for Surrendering to God

In the 13th chapter of John, verse 36, we read

"Simon Peter said, 'Master, where are You going?' and Jesus replied, 'You can't go with me now; but you will follow Me later.'"

Precious Lord, when we feel self-sufficient and think we are in charge and can handle it all, You wait and allow us finally to come to the end of our own, very limited resources. Then when we cry out to You in desperation You send us Your Holy Spirit Who empowers us to see that You are the One Who can do all things in us.

We pray in Your name, Lord Jesus!

Amen

for Surrendering to God

In Psalm 46, verses 1 - 3, & 7, we read

"God is our refuge and strength an ever-present help in trouble. Therefore we will not fear though the earth give way and the mountains fall into the heart of the sea, though its waters roar and foam and the mountains quake with their surging. The Lord Almighty is with us; the God of Jacob is our fortress."

Heavenly Father, help all of us remember that when we are in terrible, life threatening situations, You, our mighty Lord, are with us, so that we can put our trust and hope in You.

We pray in the name of God, our ever-present Help!

Amen

for Surrendering to God

In the 22nd chapter of Genesis, verse 9, we read

"Abraham built an altar there and arranged the wood on it. He bound his son Isaac and laid him on the top of the wood."

O Lord, increase our faith and love for You so that we will be able to give You our all, even the things most dear to us, as Abraham did by being willing to sacrifice his only son. Thank You for showing Abraham and us that You want us not to die but to be a living sacrifice for You each day.

We pray in Your name, mighty God!

Amen

492

for Surrendering to God

In the 26th chapter of Acts, verse 18, we read

"...to open their eyes, that they may turn from darkness and from the power of Satan to God, that they may receive forgiveness of sins and a place among those who are sanctified by faith in (Jesus)."

Precious Lord, thank You that You allow us to receive the gift of turning from evil ways and being saved by Your blood. As we realize more and more that this gift is so much help in our daily lives, we want more of You, so we strive to give up our right to ourselves and give our all to You. Thank You for the amazing grace of Your love!

We pray in Your name, Jesus our Savior!

Amen

for Surrendering to God

In the 23rd chapter of Luke, verse 26, we read

"And as they led Jesus away, they seized one Simon of Cyrene, who was coming in from the country, and laid on him the cross, to carry it behind Jesus."

Dear Lord, it seems at times that what I hear You saying to me is not what others feel is right. So will You help me to obey You and do what You want me to do no matter what others say or may suffer because of what I do? Let me trust You to take care of those who think I am wrong.

We pray in Your name, all-knowing God!

Amen

A One Minute Daily Scripture and Prayer
for Surrendering to God

In the 6th chapter of Isaiah, verse 8, we read

"Then I heard the voice of the Lord saying, 'Whom shall I send? And who will go for us?' And I said, 'Here am I. Send me!'"

Dear Lord, give us ears to hear Your voice calling to us. When You ask us to go for You, give us the courage to answer as Isaiah did and say, "Here I am Lord; send me!"

We pray in Your name, Lord!

Amen

A One Minute Daily Scripture and Prayer
for Surrendering to God

In the 9th chapter of John, verse 4A, we read

"All of us must quickly carry out the tasks assigned us by the One who sent Me."

Dear Lord, give each of us a sure knowledge of what You want us to be and to do; give us every grace we need to spend our days doing the work You have entrusted to us.

We pray in Your name, Lord Jesus!

Amen

for Surrendering to God

In the 20th chapter of Acts, verse 25, we read

"Now I know that none of you among whom I have gone about preaching will ever see me again."

O Lord, give us courage to be able to face the time when we must depart this earth, or just depart those we love for a time, and let us be at peace with whatever comes, knowing that our life is in Your hands, so all is well.

We pray in Your name, Lord Jesus Christ!

Amen

Afterword

With gratitude to God for all the people He has put into my life – those who took me to Church as a child, who taught me Sunday School, who taught me to love the Bible, who taught me to pray, who loved and supported me, and who have enriched my life by sharing their faith and friendship – I rejoice in the Lord's goodness to me, and I lift up these who are named and all those whose names remain in my heart.

Mother and Dad, Big Mama, Big Daddy, Aunt Adele, Aunt Audie, my husband Phillip Leach, Brother John Wilkins, Sr William, Dr Frank Laubach, Brother Bob Lewis and Ann, my extended Peavy, Holleman, and Leach families, Lee Bennett, Sisters Margaret, Veronica, and Jeremiah, Annie Gaspar, Fr Ralph and Terri, Dr Bradford, Dr Clendenin, Nick and Marty Sholars, Brother Andrew, friends in the Charismatic Movement, friends in the Order of St Luke, friends at First Baptist Church, First Assembly of God, First United Methodist Church, St Cyprian's Episcopal, and the Monastery of the Infant Jesus, friends: Dorothy Gockerman, Jetta, Dolly, Joy, and Martha, artists, musicians and architects whose work has brought the glory of God to me, and my dear family, Phill Jr., Les, Chrissy, and Katie.

36407091R00274

Printed in Great Britain
by Amazon